# MARKETING

**The Foundation of
Successful Business**

# MARKETING

## The Foundation of Successful Business

by Jim Foley

GUILD OF MASTER CRAFTSMAN
PUBLICATIONS LTD

This revised edition first published 1999 by
Guild of Master Craftsman Publications Ltd,
166 High Street, Lewes
East Sussex BN7 1XU

Original text first published 1992 and revised 1995

Reprinted 2002, 2003, 2004, 2006

ISBN 1 86108 124 3

A catalogue record of this book is available from the
British Library

Cover designed by Oliver Prentice
Content designed by Samantha Reeves
Edited by Peter Roper

Set in Berkeley Book and Futura

Printed and bound in the UK by St Ives.

# Contents

# Introduction

*In the beginning there was an idea – enthusiasm gave it birth, finance gave it life. Eventually it became a product, something everyone would want. Or so it was thought!*

*After a time the product died and the company failed. Everyone said it was a great idea – but it just wasn't quite what they wanted. Perhaps if it had been available in a different size or a different colour, maybe just a little bit cheaper...*

Every year numerous new products come on to the market – some succeed, and some fail. Some succeed by accident, others by design. Some fail through bad luck or bad timing, others by bad planning. That is what this book is all about: success and failure in the market place.

Marketing is not a panacea for all new or existing products. It will not make a bad product good – nor even look good. In fact good marketing can make a bad product fail faster than by doing nothing at all. By exposing a bad product to a large potential audience, its faults become obvious that much sooner and word of its shortcomings soon spreads. No, marketing is not a con trick. It's about giving customers choice.

If you have ever picked up a novel where the action takes place around the turn of the century you will find the term marketing used in a very different context than today. About a hundred years ago women used to do their marketing on a daily basis. This meant that they were going to do their shopping – choosing the products their family would use or consume in the days ahead. And consumer choice is the active ingredient in marketing today. It was Henry Ford who said that you could have any colour you like provided it was black, but that was in the early days of automobile production when the consumer had little choice but to accept what the manufacturer gave him.

Today anyone purchasing a new motor car would want to choose the colour of the car and the upholstery, the tint on the windows, and even the quality of the in-car entertainment. That's marketing for you.

Throughout this book the reader will be encouraged to look upon marketing less as a technique and more as a discipline. Not so much a collection of clever little gimmicks, more a series of planned, carefully thought out, practical procedures designed to achieve set objectives. And always with the customer in mind. For it is the customer who chooses the product, it is the customer who pays for the product, and it is the customer who ultimately decides whether the product will succeed – or fail!

This book has deliberately been written as simply as possible, to make understandable what is often made unnecessarily difficult. This is not to suggest that marketing is a simple activity – quite the reverse. Properly practised, marketing requires careful thought, detailed planning, and rigorous discipline. It is the basic concept of marketing, around which this book is written, which is deceptively simple – the idea of profitably satisfying a customer need. Neither is it a theoretical book. It does not dwell on complex reasons, nor delve deeply into why these things are important. It concentrates on the practical aspects and focuses on what needs to be done – and how to do it.

There is no right way to read this book. Some readers will want to start at the beginning and work their way through. For this purpose the sequence of chapters attempts to follow a logical structure. Others will want to read specific sections on advertising, public relations or whatever interests them most. For this purpose each chapter is entire in itself and not overly cross-referenced.

It is assumed throughout that many readers are exceptionally busy people who have little enough time to spend reading. For them there is a summary at the end of each chapter. This is provided to enable anyone who wants to, to skim through very quickly, picking out chapters and sections that are of most interest to them. They can then refer back to the detail at a later date.

Above all, this book is written for anyone with an interest in marketing. If you are puzzled why some companies are more successful than others at marketing; if you want to know why people buy one product in preference to another; or simply what marketing is and how it works, this book is for you. Hopefully you will find it helpful, informative and constructive.

# 1

# What Marketing Means

There are probably as many definitions of marketing as there are marketing textbooks. Yet many of them do little more than stress one aspect of the subject over another and most are simply variations on a single theme. If we tried to encapsulate them all in one short statement, we might say that marketing is the profitable satisfaction of a customer need. But what exactly does this mean? Surely every business is trying to make a profit and please its customers? What is so special about marketing?

Marketing is a means of profitably satisfying a customer need. It is a methodology, a process of attaining an objective, a means of achieving an end. Marketing involves setting objectives, planning campaigns, measuring progress, redefining strategy and, when that has been done, making sure it all works. And if you wanted to be really clever, you might throw in a degree of flair and imagination to top it all off.

Unfortunately, as with so many things in life, it is the tip of the iceberg, the small part above the waterline, that gets noticed most – the advertising slogan that everyone remembers, the press release that gains national publicity, the promotion that manages to break through the ordinary barrier to achieve extraordinary results – these are noticed and receive attention. But behind the creativity is a lot of hard work. Never was the description "10% inspiration, 90% perspiration" more apt than in the field of marketing achievement.

How do you get your organisation to achieve successful marketing results? You work at it, you work at it, and then you work at it some more. It cannot be stressed too many times that marketing is not a quick-fix solution to an intractable problem. Sometimes an inspired marketing response, or even a partial marketing response, can be seen to work miracles. It happens. But then someone, somewhere, is going to win the lottery. If you really want to achieve the best results in business you can't rely on luck. What you need is a

3

marketing programme that works. And this will come about when you prepare, plan, measure performance, and adjust as circumstances dictate. And you begin with a SWOT analysis.

## A SWOT Analysis

A SWOT analysis is an objective assessment of your company's Strengths, Weaknesses, Opportunities and Threats. It doesn't sound much, does it? But done properly, a SWOT analysis can be the key that opens the door on what could be many important skeletons hanging in your company closet. It's not a five-minute job, although it's tempting to look upon it that way. It requires a lot of thought and the sort of objectivity that only comes when we honestly try to look at ourselves as others see us. And many features may appear under more than one heading. For example, a high level of stock can be a strength when customers require completion of their orders quickly, but a weakness when much-needed cash is required instead – the acquisition of a customer by a larger competitor can be a threat if it is likely to result in a loss of business, but an opportunity if it leads the way to obtaining new business.

Sometimes the same business attribute can appear under all four headings – as a strength, a weakness, an opportunity and a threat. For example, the fact that you have your own fast, reliable and efficient delivery service can be seen as a strength. If, however, your competitors contract out their delivery service and provide a cheaper service than your own, it might be a weakness. Should you consider selling off or closing down your own delivery service and buying one in at a cheaper rate – that could be seen as an opportunity. However, if the new delivery service is not as fast, reliable or efficient, and replacing it with a bought-in service upsets some of your most important customers, this is most certainly a threat.

A SWOT analysis is something every company should undertake and review on a regular basis. It should consider anything and everything the company is involved in so that changes of direction, which occur in all businesses from time to time, are planned and monitored – and not just subject to drift. It should consider everything from new products to new technology, from a change in customers' purchasing power to customers' changing buying habits. An idea of just a few of the business attributes which could be featured in a SWOT analysis is shown in Figure 2.

**Figure 1**

*SWOT Analysis*

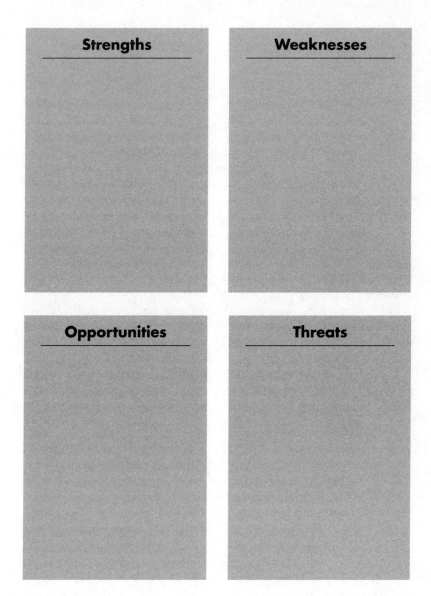

**Figure 2**

*SWOT Analysis*

| Strengths | Weaknesses |
|---|---|
| Well-known company name. | Company image a bit old-fashioned. |
| A few good and very loyal customers. | Too much work obtained from too few customers. |
| Reliable, efficient in-house delivery service. | Competitors providing cheaper contracted-out delivery service. |
| Fast, accurate estimating department. | Prices not as competitive as they should be. |
| Stock levels very high. | Too much money tied up in stock. |

| Opportunities | Threats |
|---|---|
| New product design looks very appealing. | Cost of new product launch higher than expected. |
| New industrial estate opening nearby. | Major customer moving to new site further away. |
| Cost savings to be made buying in a delivery service. | Possible customer dissatisfaction if contract delivery service bought in. |
| Interest rate cut promises cheaper overdraft. | Borrowing level still too high. |
| Major customer acquired by larger company. | Major customer acquired by larger company. |

If you are new to marketing, why not draft out a SWOT analysis for your organisation right now? You need not spend a lot of time on it at this stage, but you can add to it as you read through this book and other ideas come to you. Once you are satisfied that you have included as much as you can, you might then want to discuss it with your accountant or professional adviser. Tell him or her the story of you and your business and wait for the response. You can then redraft your SWOT analysis and consider the decisions that flow from it. For this is not just an intellectual exercise. If your analysis shows that your stock levels are too high, you should take steps to reduce them. If you believe there is an opportunity to obtain more business from the company that has just acquired one of your customers, you should be knocking on someone's door today. For despite what the proverb says, grass does not grow under feet that stand still.

A SWOT analysis is a crucial first step in the preparation of a marketing plan. And following closely behind should come a detailed study of the marketing environment.

## The Marketing Environment

No business can operate in a vacuum. Events take place outside the organisation which are totally beyond your control but nevertheless vitally affect your performance and profitability. Some of these have an impact on almost everybody and are pretty obvious. These include things like changes in tax levels or interest rates. Others are more subtle and localised, like a competitor going out of business or unexpected problems in obtaining raw materials supplies which are specific to one industry.

There are so many factors that can affect your business and they take place every day. That is why it is important for you to try and ensure that you are kept aware of them. They are reported regularly in the financial press, local newspapers or trade magazines. You may not have the time to read them in great detail but you still owe it to yourself to learn as much as you can.

Another effective and enjoyable way of keeping abreast of market developments is networking; one of the fastest growing and most beneficial activities for small businesses. Do take full advantage of trade association membership by talking to other companies just like your own. Make contact with other people in your industry or line of business; discuss market conditions with customers, suppliers and even competitors; attend lectures and meetings organised by your local Chamber of Commerce or Trade and Enterprise Council (TEC). All knowledge is power but the most powerful are those individuals with an up-to-date knowledge of their particular market.

Some of the environmental factors that could affect your business are short term, some are long term. It is not always easy to tell the difference. You would not be the first person to dismiss a new innovation as a fad or passing fancy when looking at what will later be seen as a complete change of direction in the market place. In the late 1970s IBM, one of the world's biggest, most powerful corporations, treated the development of the personal computer (PC) as nothing more than a whim, certainly no threat to their market dominance. This oversight or blind spot made IBM late entrants into what would become the fastest growth market in their history, contributing to billion dollar losses in the early '90s and very nearly destroying them. If IBM can make mistakes like this so can you! The changes that could affect you will be more easily recognised for what they are if your organisation conducts regular marketing audits.

## The Marketing Audit

Everyone knows about the financial audit: the historical assessment of a company's financial performance by a professionally qualified independent outsider. A marketing audit is similar in one way, different in another. Similar in that the financial audit attempts to assess the financial health of the company and the marketing audit tries to assess the health of its marketing activities. But different in that the marketing audit is a systematic internal appraisal and review of current marketing objectives and strategies which tries to highlight any differences or variances from the marketing plan as they occur. Its primary objective is to enable improvements to be made in the future. It will also help to identify where there are differences between what people believe to be happening and what is actually happening.

The marketing audit should also make it easier to review current performance and identify those areas where results are better or worse than expected. Unlike the financial audit which is an historical assessment of company performance, the marketing audit is ongoing and allows management to make changes that will improve profitability, even before the current marketing plan has expired.

The marketing audit takes place on two levels. In the first place it looks at changes that are taking place outside the company, within the marketing environment. It then considers the impact these changes are likely to make on the performance of the business, whether for good or ill. For example, what is the likely effect on the business if there is a change in bank interest rates, and what adjustments may be necessary to bring the marketing plan back on course?

Secondly, the marketing audit concerns itself with events happening within the business. It looks at specific performance levels and compares them (possibly by ratios or indices) with the marketing plan, making recommendations for improved performance where necessary. Some examples include: increasing sales, improving the response rate from recent direct mail campaigns, or reducing the company's dependence on specific suppliers or customers. There are many more.

Quite possibly you have never been involved in organising a marketing audit before. Perhaps you cannot quite see the need for one in your organisation. You may well be satisfied with current marketing performance and will not consider making any changes until the time draws near for the annual review. You may even feel right now that you will only make changes if dictated by budgetary constraints imposed from above. If so, you could well be missing out on many opportunities. The world around us is changing all the time. The marketing environment is changing with it. How can you possibly expect to maximise performance unless you are constantly looking for the new opportunities these changes present? There used to be a saying: "If it ain't broke – don't fix it." This does not apply today. The successful companies – and particularly the continually successful ones – are proactively seeking ways to improve every activity within their business. They are in tune with a constantly changing business environment.

Why not start making notes now on your marketing activity and performance, however limited they may be? Perhaps you do not have a sophisticated marketing plan prepared at the moment. This can come later. But there is no reason at all why you can't look at your advertising (even if it is just a card in a newsagent's window), your promotional literature (even if it is just a letterhead and a business card), your sales efforts (even if it is just you and your husband or wife making a few phone calls), and see where they could be improved and/or expanded. These are all necessary first steps in preparing a comprehensive marketing plan.

## The Marketing-Oriented Company

All businesses, in one way or another, reflect the personality of the chief executive. This does not apply only to business. You simply have to look at what happens in a school when there is a change of headteacher to know that this is true. A marketing-oriented company is invariably led by a marketing-oriented chief executive. And from him or her that marketing emphasis will permeate the whole organisation. Properly planned and implemented it should go to the very heart of the company's operations in the concern shown for the customer at every level of activity.

This is not something that applies only to salespeople. Respect for the customer is expressed in the way a telephone is answered, a letter is written, or an invoice presented. It is shown in the quality of goods and services supplied, and their delivery on the promised date. There is simply no point in telling your customers that you value their business if your receptionist is rude, your accounts department aggressive, or your deliveryman or woman inconsiderate. Drivers who deliver your products may believe that they work for your Transport Department, but if they are courteous and polite and anxious to make a good impression on all your customers, they are obviously aware of their marketing responsibilities and are working for a marketing-oriented company. And it is not only your own staff who need to be concerned with pleasing your customers. Agents, dealers and distributors too, all need to recognise their place in your marketing chain. And if you are unable to get this across to them, or your message seems to be falling on deaf ears, don't wait any longer to decide if you should have new agents, new dealers and/or new distributors for your products or services.

The business world today is tough, it's aggressive, and it should be constantly thinking of what it ought to be doing to please customers. In other words, if you can't find a way to please them, your competitors almost certainly will. No business, certainly not one that claims to be marketing biased, can allow telephones to ring unanswered, or fail to take messages and return calls. Customers' demands may be difficult to satisfy, sometimes they may even be a pain in the neck, but they are never irrelevant. And your staff should be constantly aware of this.

## Training

Training is a crucial element in any marketing programme, and an essential part of marketing communications. Without training many key members of your organisation may not appreciate the importance of their role within the company. In fact, until it is pointed out to them, they may not recognise themselves as key members and would be surprised to hear themselves described as such. But the young lady who answers your telephone most of the time, and the packer in the warehouse, as much as the sales and marketing director, should recognise the part they play in meeting customers' needs. They should understand the importance of customer contact, from the first telephone enquiry to delivery of the products ordered; from taking down an order to handling a complaint. And if they fail through lack of understanding or training, the fault may rest with the company as much as it does with them.

So often employees are heard to say: "I could do so much more – if only they would let me." Companies who are so careful to preserve and protect the manufacturing and financial assets of the company often waste the potential of their most valuable asset – their people. Only when they identify this potential, and train and empower their employees to capitalise on it, will they get the best return on the investment they have already made in human resources.

Machinery often needs to be adapted to fit a company's requirements. Computers sometimes require new software in order to respond more effectively to the demands of the purchaser. It should not be surprising therefore that employees too require training and guidance if they are to fulfil their function in the marketing chain to the satisfaction of your customers. Every person in the organisation has the potential to improve. For training to be cost effective we need to identify the personal development opportunities by reviewing the strengths and weaknesses of each individual, ensuring that the training they are to receive addresses all these opportunities. Properly targeted training not only improves effectiveness, it improves motivation.

Training may consist of sending employees on carefully selected and relevant training courses. It may be part of a professionally organised and ongoing in-house training programme. It may sometimes seem expensive. But properly planned and executed, professional training will always pay for itself in the long run. Some companies have been heard to say: "We can't afford to train our staff." Successful companies claim: "We can't afford not to train our staff."

## SUMMARY

- Marketing is a means of profitably satisfying a customer need. It is a means to an end, a process of attaining an objective, a methodology.

- Marketing begins with an analysis of a company's Strengths, Weaknesses, Opportunities and Threats. In short, a SWOT analysis.

- The marketing environment exists outside the organisation. What happens there can have an impact on sales and profits.

- A marketing audit is a systematic internal appraisal and review of current marketing objectives and strategies which tries to highlight differences or variances from the marketing plan as they occur.

- A marketing audit looks at the wider marketing environment as well as specific marketing activities inside the company.

- A marketing-oriented company places customer satisfaction at the centre of its activities.

- Key employees, whatever their position in the company, should appreciate the importance of their role within the company. They will require training and guidance if they are to fulfil their function in the marketing chain.

# What Planning Achieves

2

Business, like everything in life, contains an element of risk. Of course you can take precautions which may reduce risk. And if you think long and hard enough about your decisions beforehand, you may even manage to weigh the odds in your favour and thus increase your chances of getting the result you want. But you can never eliminate risk entirely. In fact you might even say that in business the greatest risk is not taking any risks at all.

One thing that will help enormously is to try and accumulate as much information and as many facts as possible. In fact the more information you have, the more facts that are available, the more likely you are to make the right decision. If possible you should try to develop a structure where you are being fed relevant information continuously. However, a word of caution. Information costs money, even if calculated simply in the time taken to collect it. When the cost of collection comes closer to the value of any savings you are likely to make, the information you obtain is worth less and less. And if you look closely enough at yourself you may find that your need for more facts may well hide a subconscious desire for inaction. Facts and information should help you make decisions, not avoid them.

Preparation is vital and anyone involved in marketing should realise this. Preparation promotes anticipation, and it is always prudent to anticipate problems and difficulties before they arise. For example, careful thought and preparation in the planning stage of a project may well anticipate the need for investment and measure the likely return on that investment. And in business today there are few more profitable investments you can make than taking the time and trouble to prepare a proper marketing plan. After all, if you are involved in manufacturing you do not walk into the factory every morning without having a very clear idea of what products you are going to produce that day, and in what quantities. Quite probably you will also have a production board showing what you plan to produce not just for the day, or even the week, but possibly the months ahead as well. And in the midst of your schedules you will also have taken time out for holidays and other foreseen circumstances. That is planning. Why then would you choose to plan your production but not the process that ensures your products are sold rather than left to clutter up the dark recesses of some warehouse or other?

Some will say, and even believe, that marketing planning is tiresome and boring, an unnecessary expenditure of valuable resources which could be better employed in making products or providing a service. But observe the construction of a tall building. It doesn't start on the top floor. It starts well below ground, in the foundations that no one will ever see. Work on these foundations takes time, a lot of effort, and probably a great deal of money too. Clearing the site, digging the base, getting it level, making sure that it's firm –

---

## Case History

*In his book* Making It Happen, *John Harvey Jones talks about the Japanese commitment to planning, and how they take time to involve people at every level of the organisation.*

*However, when the time for action comes – they are able to move like lightning. He tells the story of how ICI licensed a process to the Japanese which involved both parties simultaneously building parazylene plants – one on Teesside and the other in Japan. ICI seconded an engineer to work with their design team and to act as co-ordinator between the two projects.*

*After four months, John Harvey Jones's team were already breaking ground and congratulating themselves for being well ahead of the Japanese who, the engineer told them, were still in the planning stage! The outcome of this story is that, to the horror of John Harvey Jones and his team, the Japanese completed their plant seven months before the British team – and in addition, it operated at the first press of the button, whilst the British plant took a further three months in troubleshooting and teething problems. John Harvey Jones would agree with us: planning pays off – in production and in marketing.*

---

it all takes a lot of work. But once it's done, the rest of the building goes up easily and quickly. The punch line is: the best plans are always built on solid foundations.

One thing that should be stressed, however, is that a marketing plan is not a blueprint. It's more a travel guide that keeps you pointing in the direction you want to go. It should also tell you when and where you are going wrong, thus enabling you to take the necessary corrective action. It begins by looking at your company and what your company does.

## What Business Are You In?

It has been said that the demise of the large independent railway companies that dominated the United States business world at the end of the nineteenth century was caused by their inability to understand the business they were in. They thought they were in the railroad business when, in fact, they were in the transportation business. Unfortunately this is an oversimplification.

It could just as easily be claimed that the railways went out of business because their management refused to accept change and showed a remarkable lack of willingness to recognise the need for it when it was staring them in the face. But it is a fact that those few railway companies who did realise that they were not permanently trapped within the narrow confines of their own industry, and consequently did expand into sea and air transportation, survived and prospered.

Consider how this might apply to your business. Are you, for example, involved in publishing or the dissemination of information? If the former you might be inclined to restrict your business activities to the production of books and magazines. If the latter you might look further afield at the demand for audio cassettes, compact discs and videos, and respond accordingly.

Then again, are you a builder or are you involved in home improvements? If the former you might confine your activities to building houses and extensions planned and initiated by the home owner. If the latter you would almost certainly ensure that you have access to the latest information concerning new bathroom fittings, kitchen units and conservatories, amongst others. It all depends how far you are prepared to go. And that is very dependent on how you see your company and its future.

## Looking at Yourself

Self-criticism is not easy. Too much can even be harmful and destructive. Taken to extremes it can lead to exaggerated beliefs concerning competitors' abilities and your own inability. This is self-defeating. (See final section in this chapter.) Constructive criticism is what we should be concerned with, and if we are prepared to look at our faults and recognise them for what they are, we can then go on to find ways of correcting them.

*Q. Does your company treat customers as you wish to be treated by someone else?*

One of the best things those in business can do is to look periodically at their company as if they were a new or potential customer. Supposing you were to do this – objectively speaking, what do you think you would find? Would you notice that the telephones were answered promptly and pleasantly? Would you find that your queries were dealt with quickly and efficiently? And what about complaints? Would you say that they were taken seriously and handled sympathetically? In short, looking at your company today, do you feel that it treats your customers as you would wish to be treated by someone else? You shouldn't avoid the question nor fudge the answer.

*Q. Does your stationery etc., project the image you are seeking?*

The first contact a potential customer has with your business is probably through an advertisement, a leaflet or letter of introduction. What does he or she find? Is yours a company that has kept up with the times and looks to be energetic and youthful in its approach? Or is it more old-fashioned, exuding an image of experience and maturity? Either one is fine – but only for the right business. If your stationery looks as though it was designed in 1928 there is no way you can appear young and vigorous. If instead it appears brash and colourful it's unlikely to make you seem old and dependable. And if it's badly designed and printed, in any style, you are probably giving the impression of being cheap and shoddy as well.

*Q. Do you respond quickly and efficiently to all written customer contact?*

Assuming a new or potential customer contacts your company by letter, how promptly is it answered? Could a reply be expected in two or three days, a week, or even longer? Does it depend on who is available to respond? It could be a quick response when you are around but what happens if you are sick or on holiday? Does someone write a holding letter explaining that the complaint/query/estimate request or whatever will be dealt with by you on your return? Or is the customer left hanging in the air, left to wonder if a reply will ever be forthcoming? Answer as honestly as you can.

*Q. Is the telephone always answered in a quick,*
*efficient and friendly manner?*

And if the initial contact is by telephone, how is it answered? Is it prompt? Is it polite? And what happens if the caller can't be put through immediately and has to be placed on hold? Are they left in silence, not knowing whether they are still connected or if they have been cut off? Or do they have to listen to the same tune played over and over again until driven close to madness, suicide or both? Telephone answering is important. A pharmaceutical company in Berkshire was usually so quick to answer the telephone that regular callers knew that they had to be alert and ready with their requests. As a result, very little time was wasted and all calls went through quickly. A printer in Sussex has been subjecting callers placed on hold to the same dirge for so long that even their own salespeople grit their teeth before calling in.

Looking at your company as a new or potential customer can be a very constructive exercise. It can also be rewarding. For, as stressed initially, this should be a constructive exercise. Not everything in your company is wrong otherwise you wouldn't still be in business.

It can be as gratifying to identify what you are doing well as it is necessary to understand what you are doing badly. And it pays to be thorough. You should begin at the beginning and follow right through from submitting an estimate, meeting the customer and checking the quality of the service or products provided, to invoicing, payment and follow-up. You might even give each department marks or grades so that future reviews will show if overall performance is improving or deteriorating.

## Looking at Your Competitors

Whilst looking at your own business, it usually helps to look at the competition. There are dangers in this as well. As mentioned earlier it is very easy to exaggerate the strengths of your competitors and become demoralised as a result (see case study page 20). But if you can remain reasonably objective and gauge competitors' strengths and weaknesses on a similar scale to your own, it can be more than just a helpful exercise. In particular it can be useful when deciding whether or not to implement a price increase. For if others are providing a lesser service at higher prices whilst still obtaining sufficient work, perhaps you can safely increase your prices without the risk of losing too many of your own customers. However, it is important that your judgements are as objective as possible and supported by independent third-party observations wherever possible.

---

### Case Study

*During the Second World War, when General Montgomery took over the Eighth Army in the desert, he soon realised that one of his first tasks was to lift the morale of the men serving under him. Demoralised and dejected they had come to believe that Field Marshal Rommel, who commanded the German troops, was invincible. General Montgomery issued a statement reminding his men that Rommel was only human, that he made mistakes, that he could be beaten, and that the British troops were the ones to do it. Inspired by Montgomery's assurances, freshly motivated by a new belief in themselves, and now convinced that the enemy was not all-powerful, the Eighth Army then went on to victory.*

---

*Checking the competition*

## SUMMARY

- In business you may be able to weigh the odds in your favour but you can never eliminate risk entirely.

- Facts and information increase the probability of making the right decision, but they do cost money.

- Accumulating facts and information should never be an excuse for inaction.

- Marketing planning, like production planning, is essential for the development and growth of the company.

- The best plans are those which have been well prepared and well researched.

- The business you are in may not be quite as narrow and confining as you first think.

- It helps to look at your business through the eyes of your customers at every point of contact.

- It should be possible to measure your performance and make periodic checks for signs of improvement or otherwise.

- Competitors' performance may also be evaluated on the same scale and compared directly with your own.

- Judgement of competitors' performance should be objective and supported by independent third-party observation wherever possible.

# Types of Marketing

3

One has only to pick up any of a number of marketing textbooks today to realise that there are numerous varieties of marketing currently in vogue. Pick any adjective, add the word 'marketing' and it all seems to fit: relationship marketing, lifestyle marketing, database marketing – the list is endless. And provided that the description aids understanding, all well and good. Where, however, the multiplication of marketing concepts is nothing more than a combination of different sales approaches, confusion follows and marketing is made to seem unnecessarily complicated and difficult.

This is not to say that different approaches to the various aspects of marketing are not sometimes necessary and highly desirable. Because we, as individuals, are very different and have individual ways of expressing our need for the same or similar products, any manufacturer or distributor attempting to sell these products must find different ways of marketing to us. That's common sense. For example, consider a car dealer selling the same model car to me, as an individual, and to you, as a car hire company. He or she will emphasise certain features of the car to me, and different features entirely to you. In both cases, though, that person will be attempting to satisfy our individual needs. It is only because our needs vary that these different approaches are adopted. Nor does it end there. Whereas the initial approach to me could have come through a newspaper, perhaps, or a Sunday supplement; the point of contact with you is more likely to have been through a trade magazine or even a personal call from a sales representative. Different markets require dedicated messages and selected media. And before commencing any marketing programme, both the medium and the message have to be considered in the light of the potential customers we are trying to reach.

## Consumer Marketing

Most of us, when talking of consumer marketing, think in terms of mass markets: regular viewers of *Coronation Street*, the total readership of the *Daily Mirror* and the like.

This is a misconception. Advertising to consumers can be localised and personal if the value of the purchase warrants it. A salesman selling encyclopedias door-to-door or an estate agent you have approached about buying a house will be perfectly happy, in fact may well prefer, trying to sell to you on a one-to-one basis. And, in a similar vein, the companies who employ them will have designed their marketing strategies precisely around this approach. But even where the purchase is less valuable than a house or a set of encyclopedias, it is still possible to direct your marketing to small groups of consumers. A mailshot selling a specialist product to a select group of householders, an advertisement in a small specialist magazine, perhaps even your local church newsletter – all of these come under the heading of consumer marketing.

The message, too, can be as varied as the potential size of the audience. A distributor of swimming pool supplies may choose a selected mailshot over an advertisement in a local newspaper because he or she will find it easier directing the sales message to those households in the area most likely to possess their own pool. The total audience may be considerably smaller but the cost of reaching individual prospective customers will be lower because there is far less wastage. In addition, as a piece of sales literature, the sales message will be more personal and direct, and much more informative than an advertisement in a newspaper or magazine, or even a 30-second television commercial.

The cost of advertising to consumers varies greatly as well. It is important therefore to distinguish between aggregate or total cost and the individual cost, or cost per thousand. The larger the audience the lower cost per thousand you should pay, but the higher the aggregate cost. For example a leaflet mailed to households will cost around £250 a thousand for postage alone depending upon the level of discount received – and that does not include any of the production or mailing costs. On the other hand, a full page full colour advertisement in *The Sun* will cost around £12 a thousand. Quite a difference. However, the total costs may be just as different in the other direction. It would take quite an extensive direct mail campaign to cost more than the £46,600 you could be charged for taking a full page full colour advertisement in Britain's most popular daily newspaper.

The decision on how best to market your product or service to consumers will therefore depend upon many factors, not least of which may be the nature of the product or service itself. This is something you may have to reflect upon quite seriously if you have previously marketed only to industry or business but now believe your product or service to have consumer appeal. What you have to bear in mind is that some products lend themselves more to mass marketing – usually where a short and possibly simple message adequately conveys the nature of the product to potential customers – whereas others require a more personal approach. Most of all the choice revolves around targeting and wastage. The size of the total audience may sound impressive but matters less than the number of potential purchasers – those actually able and likely to buy. And this applies as much to a quarter-page black and white advertisement in the local church newsletter as it does to a full colour page in *The Sun*.

## Industrial Marketing

As a rule, orders for industrial products are larger and more complicated than purchases made by consumers. The needs of industry are very different than those of most consumers, most of the time. By way of example, think of a businessman or woman buying a calculator for home or office use. At home a quite simple machine would probably suffice: something with the four basic arithmetic functions and quite a small memory. For the office though a much more complicated machine would be required: one with statistical functions, a large memory and, perhaps, compatibility with a personal computer. And where the needs of the market are different so too should be the marketing.

The industrial customer is also very different from the average consumer. Industrial purchases are more likely to be objective, considered and dispassionate. Buyers working for large industrial concerns often work to strict budgets within very tight constraints, and are frequently called upon to justify their purchasing decisions – especially when something goes wrong. This means that the industrial buyer is more likely to be swayed by facts rather than by any emotional feelings, and to consider the long-term cost implications more than any short-term satisfaction.

In addition, it has to be remembered that the industrial buyer is rarely buying something for him or herself. Others specify their needs, dictate their conditions and can, on occasion, become involved in the decision-making process. An alert sales representative will be aware of this. The role of the sales representative will be discussed in more detail later (see Chapter 8: Selling the Product) but something should be said here about the nature of selling to the industrial buyer.

Personal selling is an interactive process. It allows the purchaser to ask difficult or technical questions and the sales representative to respond to them. The position of the sales representative in industrial marketing is therefore a very important one. However, personal selling is very expensive. The cost of making a call, must include the time taken to drive to and from the customer, allow for travel and entertaining expenses plus the support of ancillary staff in the sales office, in addition to the remuneration of the sales person. That is why the quality of representation is so important for companies marketing to industrial customers.

## Retail Marketing

Retailers sell many products. You have only to look around a supermarket, or even the shelves of your local newsagent, to appreciate this. And if the retailer is not expected to know everything about every one of them, he or she is certainly expected to know enough about most of them to help the customer decide which product to choose.

The retailer is a middleman. His or her position in the marketing chain is usually between the wholesaler and the consumer, sometimes between the manufacturer and the consumer. In either case, he or she receives sales messages from lots of different sources and is then expected to relay them to a large number of people, all with varying needs. Quite a tall order. It is therefore incumbent upon anyone involved in selling products through the retail trade to give as much support to the retailer as possible.

This help can come in a number of ways. Many retailers are not involved in selling to their customers personally. In fact, more than ever today, consumers make their choices while the products are still on the retailers' shelves. Even quite expensive products can be purchased in this way. This means that instead of relying upon the retailer to 'push' his or her products to the customers, the manufacturer can help by 'pulling' them through the retailer. This can be done by creating a demand for them. This demand can be the result of consumer advertising, extra discounts for the retailer, allowing him or her to reduce prices without sacrificing margin, or point-of-sale material which encourages the consumer to ask for the products directly off the shelf.

For any of these promotions to work properly it is essential that the retailer has sufficient stock on hand to meet the forecast demand. He or she will usually be encouraged to increase stock by visits from manufacturers' or wholesalers' sales representatives, or advertisements featured in relevant trade magazines.

## Export Marketing

Marketing campaigns that work well in one country do not necessarily achieve the same results elsewhere in the world without making substantial changes to them. This is hardly surprising. Tastes, attitudes and social customs are rarely transportable across cultural boundaries. And both tradition and religious practice, which greatly influence dress codes, diet, and even thought processes, can change dramatically from one country to another – sometimes even within the same one.

When visiting another country, if we have any sensitivity or concern for the feelings of others, we attempt as far as we can to understand their customs and beliefs so as not to cause offence. It is no more than common decency. And that is why considerable thought and preparation are necessary before attempting to market our products or services to another country.

The history of marketing is full of horrendous mistakes made by companies who thought they could sell their products overseas without local knowledge and professional advice. No language is literally translatable into another without humorous or tragic consequences; religious symbols mean different things to different people and even colours which have happy associations in one culture can mean completely the reverse in the other.

Sometimes even the product name can let us down. General Motors' car the Nova can mean 'star' in some cultures, 'new' in others, but in some Spanish speaking countries it means 'doesn't go'. Hardly the best and most apt description to apply to a new car.

Apart from cultural taboos, there are many legal restrictions and trade and tariff barriers erected by governments and, as we all know, governments can change their minds quickly, and often. It therefore makes sense to consult experts in the field of export marketing who know the pitfalls, are up to date with current legislation, and have more than a passing knowledge of the local language – and its many nuances. Those who do not, stand the risk of making the same mistake as the English company selling in Finland, as described in the case study below.

## Case Study

*A Rose by Another Name?*

*A few years ago an English company was planning a mailing to a large number of homes in Finland. Unfortunately, in translating the text, the Finnish letter 'Ø', with a slash, became the English letter 'O', without one, changing the meaning of one word quite dramatically. Instead of being offered the holiday home of a lifetime, Finnish consumers found that they were being given the opportunity to purchase a very private part of the body.*

*The error was widely broadcast in the Finnish media, but the advertiser had the last laugh. A follow-up mailing, boldly stating 'As featured on tv' more than doubled the anticipated response.*

## SUMMARY

- Different marketing techniques are required for selling the same products to industrial and consumer markets.

- Consumer marketing is not necessarily the same thing as mass marketing.

- When considering marketing costs think of targeting and wastage. What you should be looking for is the number of potential purchasers not the total audience of one particular advertising medium.

- Industrial customers usually require more technical information than most consumers.

- The role of the sales representative is particularly important in industrial marketing.

- Retailers sell many products, receive sales messages from many different sources, and cannot be expected to know everything there is to know about every product stocked.

- To get the best from retailers, assistance should be provided when attempting to sell products through retail outlets.

- There are many potential pitfalls to be avoided when marketing products overseas.

- Tastes, attitudes and social customs, legal restrictions and trade and tariff barriers must all be considered when marketing in other countries.

# The Market

4

A highly motivated and somewhat aggressive sales manager of a large garment-manufacturing company used to have a big sign attached to the wall behind his desk which no visitor could ignore. In big, bold letters it read: "NOTHING HAPPENS UNTIL SOMEBODY SELLS SOMETHING". The purpose of it was to convince all and sundry of his commitment to the task of selling in the marketplace. And it worked. Salesmen and non-salesmen alike would leave his office fully charged up and inspired by his commitment to the company and its products. But was he right? In a sense he was, because although business activity begins with an idea, nothing really happens until that idea has been sold to someone. For the moment, though, we will not be concentrating on the selling process itself (that follows later in Chapter 8, Selling the Product), but focusing instead on the someone who is being sold to – in other words, the market. What we are looking for is a market which will be receptive to the product or service we are trying to sell.

## Identifying a Need

There is an old marketing adage which says that when someone goes into a store to buy a drill, he or she does not actually need a drill – but they do require a hole. Another way of looking at it is to say that the sum total of everyone who requires a hole represents at least part of the market for a drill. Or, to put it in yet another way, the market for any particular drill is made up, in part, by the number of people who need a hole.

Needs are not the same thing as demands although one may follow the other. For example, in the 1950s and 1960s it was the need for warm homes, rather than warm rooms heated by individual fires, which created the demand for central heating. It certainly was not a need for central heating as such because most people, up until that time, were totally unaware of its existence or availability. But those who were quick to recognise the extent of the demand, when it was manifested – equipment manufacturers, power companies, plumbers, electricians and the like – organised themselves accordingly and reaped their just rewards.

Psychologists will tell you that we all have a hierarchy of needs. They begin with the basics – the need for food, shelter and clothing – and progress through a series of certain definite and definable steps to dishwashers, videos and compact disc players – which most of us would recognise today as luxury goods.

The same thing also applies to business needs. These tend to vary through every stage of a company's development. For example in the early stages of a business the need for office equipment and furniture may be minimal. A sole trader business operating out of an old workshop or garage may not even see the need for a typewriter in the very first days of its operation. Yet years later when that same business has grown much larger, perhaps become a household name, it would be impossible to imagine it operating at all without computers on all desks, company cars issued to every member of the sales force, and fax machines available to all staff for quick and easy communications.

## Identifying a Market

How do we identify a market? A market is a group of potential customers with a single, identifiable need. Customers come in three sizes: small, medium and large. At one extreme are the heavy or regular users of your products; at the other are the light or infrequent purchasers. Recognising the difference between them could be important for your marketing efforts.

It is frequently claimed that 80% of the purchases of any particular product come from just 20% of the customers. This is called the Pareto principle or the 80/20 rule. Similarly 80% of the sales made by any one company are said to be made to 20% of their customers. This ratio is not supposed to be an exact figure. For some companies it might be 70/20, for others 60/25, but as a guiding principle it makes sense. Because of it, many companies concentrate their marketing efforts on heavy purchasers of their products. For despite all the temptations posed by selling to a new or virgin market, it is generally believed that it is easier to sell something to those who are already heavily committed to the product than it is to break new ground with infrequent purchasers or those who have never bought before. It is the same principle that persuades charities to seek donations from those who have given frequently in the past, especially when an emergency or disaster in some part of the world requires prompt and effective action.

Direct mail advertisers in particular know that on the whole they get a bigger response from those who have purchased by mail order in the past than they will from those who have yet to be convinced that direct mail is quick and efficient, and operated by reliable and trustworthy companies. That is why many companies not only go to great lengths to build up a database of their existing customers but will often buy in lists of direct mail purchasers of other, sometimes – though not always – complementary products.

It is worth mentioning at this point that there is more than a pedantic difference between a customer and a consumer. A customer is someone who buys a product, a consumer is someone who uses (or consumes) it. They are not necessarily the same person. Examples include the industrial buyer who purchases materials that are used in the manufacture of other products, retailers who buy products which later they sell on to their customers, and even the busy mother purchasing groceries for her family. In each case it is often the customer's perception of the eventual consumer's needs which most influences the buying decision. The only way to circumvent this barrier is to appeal over the head of the customer directly to the consumer. Manufacturers of children's toys often do this, attempting to influence the child to pressure the parent to buy what he or she wants. Manufacturers of industrial products also do it when they appeal directly to the end user so that their components are mentioned when industrial specifications are provided to the buyer.

## Segmenting a Market

Segmentation is one of the key concepts in marketing. It is the driving force behind niche marketing and many other ideas that have come in and gone out of vogue in recent years. But why would anyone want to segment or cut up a market anyway? At first sight it seems strange and illogical. Surely the idea is to go after as many customers as possible? Well, in a way yes, in another way no. It is true that every manufacturer wants volume. This is what keeps costs low and, by implication, profits high. And it would work very well if all customers wanted the same thing. But customers are a perverse lot. They get bored easily, they want to be different from their neighbours, they want variety. Most of the time they are simply not prepared to adjust their needs just to improve the efficiency of a production line. And that's where market segmentation comes in.

Markets can be segmented in many different ways. For example, a cabinetmaker supplying fitted furniture units to individual households might discover, purely by chance, an unexpectedly high demand for his or her skills at the top end of the market, in the higher income bracket. Because of this he or she might concentrate a direct mail campaign to the most exclusive homes in the area. This is an example of market segmentation.

A much more complicated example might be that of a brewer contemplating the introduction of a new beer. Would it be possible, do you think, to produce a beer that would appeal to all beer drinkers? Hardly! As we all know, the beer market is not homogeneous. There are those who like dark beer and others who choose light beer. There are those who like strong beer and some who, for one reason or another, ask for beer that has little or no alcohol at all. Some beer drinkers prefer a sweet taste and others like bitter. The differences are many and varied. How does the brewer decide which beer to make?

First of all the brewer has to decide how the market may be segmented. Apart from the more obvious ones which concentrate on the physical characteristics of the product itself, there are many variations within the beer drinking market itself.

For example, it could be made up of young and old, male and female; those with larger than average incomes and those with less; those who drink beer in public houses and those who drink at home – and many, many more. All these market segments can be recognised as loyal to different types of beer and great skill is required in separating them.

We might find that the market for high-strength, sweet-tasting light beers is mostly male, aged 30–45, with above average income, and just as likely to drink at home as in a public house.

On the other hand, the market for bitter-tasting, dark beers of average strength might be predominantly male, aged 45–60, with less than average income, who only drink in a public house. These are somewhat simplified hypothetical examples but, if true, what would they tell us? What they should tell us is whether a particular market segment is growing, static or contracting; whether it is full of competitive brands or open to exploitation; and whether it is worth pursuing or leaving alone. Only when the beer market has been investigated in this way would the brewer be in a position to decide on the characteristics of the beer to be launched, the likely profitability of the market segment selected, and the advertising and promotional bias likely to appeal to the target market.

It is important to note that the criteria for segmentation must be relevant to the buying decision. It might be possible to identify every potential customer who is left-handed, but it would be pointless to do so if left-handedness made no difference whatsoever to the buying decision. Nor is there anything to be gained if promotional contact is difficult or there are too many problems supplying the target market with the product. Remember that the segment chosen must be of sufficient size to warrant the attention and effort required to reach it.

## Market Segmentation

Having identified your market segments, it makes sense to evaluate them to determine which are the niche or most attractive areas for your product or service. This can be done simply by listing a number of factors which are key to the success of your business and giving a rating out of 10 to each factor, producing a total for each market segment (10 is excellent – 1 is poor).

*Clearly, market segment 3 is the one to be addressed, but you need to invest in your ability to respond and recognise that success will come from high volume, low margin sales.*

| Key Success Factors | MARKET SEGMENTS | | | |
|---|---|---|---|---|
| | 1 | 2 | 3 | 4 |
| Sales Potential | 2 | 6 | 9 | 4 |
| Minimum Competition | 3 | 4 | 8 | 2 |
| Market Growing | 6 | 5 | 9 | 2 |
| Sensitivity To Price | 2 | 4 | 3 | 3 |
| Geographically Available | 8 | 2 | 6 | 8 |
| Potential Sales / Client Ratios | 8 | 6 | 6 | 5 |
| Our Ability To Respond | 5 | 5 | 2 | 5 |
| Total | 34 | 32 | 43 | 29 |

When organised properly, the benefits of segmentation can be considerable. They reduce competition, create closer identity with the customers and increase the opportunity to make bigger profits.

## Case Study

*A few years ago a member of a well-known trade association wrote in, requesting help with the composition of a direct mail letter. The member's business was welding but, almost by accident, he had discovered a special demand he could satisfy: the manufacture of boarding kennels for animals. Those he made were secure, light and airy, and guaranteed to return a happy pet to a satisfied owner. He very soon realised that animal boarding kennels represented a major market segment which he could identify and target. With this knowledge it was quite a simple matter of writing a direct mail letter, aimed specifically at the target market, opening the door on a number of new business opportunities.*

*Another member of the same association, a plumber, also requested help with writing a direct mail letter. The market segment he identified consisted of neighbours who had small jobs they required doing which would not be attractive to larger competitors. He knew where these potential customers lived. Distribution was therefore easy, once the letter was written, advising them of his interest in their type of work.*

## SUMMARY

- Customer needs are not the same as demands although one may follow the other.

- Needs vary according to the individual. Business needs also go through many different stages as the company grows and expands.

- As a rough guide, 80% of your orders will come from 20% of your customers.

- It is usually easier to make sales to committed users of the product.

- Customers make purchases on behalf of consumers in anticipation of their perceived needs. Manufacturers sometimes circumvent this barrier by appealing directly to consumers.

- Markets can be segmented in many different ways. Great skill may be needed to identify and separate them.

- The criteria for segmentation must be relevant to the buying decision.

- When organised properly, the benefits of segmentation can be considerable.

# The Product

5

The same sales manager mentioned at the beginning of the last chapter had a second sign hanging on his office wall. It was a picture of a salesman selling his wares from the back of a horse-driven cart, laden with goods. Underneath, in big, capital letters, it boldly declared: "YOU CAN'T DO BUSINESS FROM AN EMPTY WAGON". A salesman's cry from the heart if ever there was one.

This is not really the place to argue for or against higher or lower stock levels, nor even to suggest ways and means of determining what should be the optimum stock level for any one company or any one industry. Suffice to say that without a product or service to sell, there would be no business. The whole purpose of business is to make and sell products at a higher price than the cost of making and selling them.

But what exactly do we mean by product? A product is much more than its physical characteristics – the nuts and bolts that hold it together. Every product is a package: a package that includes its price, availability, reputation, and quite a lot more.

Because we find it easier to make comparisons in numerical terms and every product has a value, we often make the mistake of thinking that all buying decisions are dictated by price alone. Admittedly we would normally expect to sell more of something if we lowered its price and less if we increased it, but even this is not always true.

Believe it or not, it is possible to price too low as well as too high. (See the following chapter: Pricing the Product.) But if you still have doubts as to whether products are bought on price alone, you need look no further than Rolls-Royce or Harrods – companies that thrive and prosper yet never deliberately set out to price below the competition.

Every product is more than the sum of its physical parts. The moment a brand name is stamped upon it, a product changes – some might say for the better, others the reverse. It all depends upon your own belief system and how it relates to that particular brand name. Time after time, blind tests – where the consumer is asked to rate the quality of products which have had the brand names removed – show different results to open tests where the brand names are clearly visible.

The added ingredient, the key element that determines whether or not the consumer prefers one product over another, is the brand image, whether it is good, bad or indifferent.

## What Are We Selling?

Sales managers are often heard encouraging their sales representatives to "sell the sizzle and not the steak". This is good marketing advice. What they are being encouraged to sell are the attributes of the product rather than the product itself. This applies in many different trades.

A used-car salesman might sell the prospect of the open road more than the car, a white goods salesman might sell the idea of constantly fresh food rather than the refrigerator itself – there are many different examples. And the one thing they all have in common is that they are expressing ways in which their products can satisfy a customer need. Whenever we attempt to market a product we should think of the requirements of our customers and ways in which our products can satisfy them.

Let's take a specific example of a couple trying to make up their minds whether or not they should buy a new fitted kitchen and, if so, from whom. Before making a decision they would almost certainly go through a particular thought and discussion process. And the most obvious place to start would be to ask themselves if they really need a new fitted kitchen at all.

The instant answer would almost certainly be yes, wondering how they had managed so long with an old, out-of-date kitchen. After some serious thought could be the question of whether or not a new kitchen deserved to take priority over the new garage planned to be purchased next. But after a period of time, having discussed all the options and having decided to go ahead and buy the new kitchen, they might well ask themselves how much they could afford to spend, what appliances to include, and whether or not everything could be included in one complete package deal. In particular, it might be suggested that the 15-year-old boiler, would be out of place in a new kitchen and be better replaced by one with all the latest bells and whistles. The timescale required to prepare, plan and fit the kitchen – whether it would be realistic to expect it to be completed and installed before Christmas – and how long the inevitable disruption and mess would last, requires serious thought. All these questions need to be answered, and the way the potential purchaser responds to the answers forms part of that continuing process we usually refer to as consumer buyer behaviour.

Which company do you think is most likely to obtain this particular order? There are a lot of choices. In the area where this fictitious (but nevertheless typical) example lives there are many companies that supply fitted kitchens. And no doubt many of these could meet the standards of quality, service and price required. But only one of them will best meet the requirements for a kitchen that falls within the budget, fitted with the appliances required (including the new boiler) in the right colour and finish, with generous payments terms, and fitted and installed before Christmas by skilled, efficient, neat, tidy and considerate craftsmen. That, in its entirety, is the product the customers want to buy.

## Enhancing the Product

In the previous chapter we gave quite a lot of attention to the idea of segmenting a market and the opportunities available to those who successfully achieved this. One method of segmenting a market which we did not discuss involves enhancing the product, or adding value to it. In other words, making the product appear different, or superior, to the competition.

A product can be enhanced by adding extra features. An example of this might be the inclusion of air conditioning or a CD player in a standard model motor car. Another way is to use improved ingredients or better quality materials. We see this most often in advertising and promotional campaigns for washing powders, cake mixes and similar products.

But there are other means of enhancement which do not involve changing the physical characteristics of the product. These might include the warmth and friendliness of your employees when answering the telephone, the helpfulness and courtesy of your sales team when called upon to offer advice, or simply the accuracy and speed of response of your estimating department. You should also remember that value is added to a product when concessionary repayment terms, discounted bonus 'gifts', or faster settlement terms are offered.

What is being suggested here is not that all these features should be provided or that some of them should form part of every standard package offered to your customers.

What has to be remembered is that the products or services being sold do not exist in isolation. They are not bought and sold on their physical characteristics alone – however attractive they may be. They are part and parcel of a whole package of benefits. And the more these benefits correspond to the needs of your customers, the more successful you will be in selling them.

## Changing the Product

Everything in life is cyclical – or so it seems. Plants and animals are born; they live for a while, and they die. The same thing happens to products. We have seen it all before. Fashions change, new products capture the imagination.

Marketing textbooks describe this as the 'Product Life Cycle'. It begins with the introduction of the product and its acceptance in the marketplace. This is usually a period of rapid growth. Sales then stabilise as the product reaches maturity and the market becomes saturated. Finally, for any number of reasons, the product goes into decline and eventually disappears. Birth, life, death – it's the way of the world.

Some products, though, last longer than others. A bit like people really. They have longer life cycles. One example which is probably most relevant to us today is the petrol-driven motor car. It was born somewhere towards the end of the 19th century and, in modern day terms, took quite a long time to get going. Yet there was almost certainly an instant demand for the product. There just wasn't a great demand for it at the price it was then being offered. It took Henry Ford and his automated assembly line to manufacture cars which the average man could afford to buy. This was in the years between the wars when sales really began to take off. But there was a hiccup – the Depression of the 1930s. Sales faltered and did not recover until after the Second World War. And now, today?

There are many who would claim that the market for petrol-driven cars, certainly in the West, has reached saturation point. The question is, will the car go into decline and, if so, when? Most people would probably agree that there are two threats to the continued existence of the petrol-driven car and when they coincide it may very well become a thing of the past. The first is the threat the car itself currently poses to the environment and the other is the introduction of an as yet uninvented replacement vehicle powered by a different source of energy. One of these is with us today, the other may not arrive for a number of years. But when it does – difficult as it may be to believe – the life cycle of the car as we know it will be over and it will very soon become as obsolete as the horse and cart.

**Typical Life Cycle Graph**

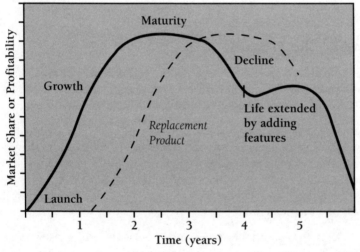

*The replacement product or service should be planned and launched before the existing product reaches maturity.*

But does the same thing apply to services as well as products? Do services have life cycles of their own? Most certainly they do. Do barbers give shaves any more? A few might. Do hotels still turn down beds in the evening? Some do, but most gave up the practice a long time ago. And even when the demand for a particular service remains, it can still go through many changes. Men's hairdressers are a case in point. They have been with us for many years and, on the premise that men will continue to want to have their hair cut on a regular basis, are likely to do so far into the future. Yet there was a time during the 1960s and 70s when men's hairdressers looked particularly vulnerable to a long-haired fashion that forced many of them out of business. And most of those who remained had to make major changes in the way they worked. Who can say what will happen to fashion in men's hair styling in the future?

In order to survive, every business has to adapt to new and changing times. The really successful businesses, however, not only see the changes happening they seize the opportunities change brings. When the sales of automatic washing machines began to accelerate many years ago, an entrepreneurial plumber would have seen what was happening, grasped the opportunity, and advised all households in his area of the excellent service he could provide in plumbing them in. If he had had more foresight than most he might also have approached the management of shops selling white goods in his locality, offering his services to customers thinking of purchasing an automatic washing machine. You can just imagine what this would mean to sales people in the store. How much easier it would be for them to sell the product with the added benefit of a reputable and reliable plumber in the wings, willing and able to plumb in the new automatic washing machines they were trying to sell, for an agreed fixed price.

The life of any product or service can be extended by adding features or benefits and the point in time when these will be added are pre-planned by most successful organisations.

Also, being prepared to change a product or service in response to customer needs is essential for any business which wants to grow and prosper.

## SUMMARY

● A product is much more than the sum of its physical parts.

● Every product or service is a package of benefits which include its price, availability, reputation, and quite a lot more.

● Products and services are rarely purchased on price alone.

● Product enhancement is a means of segmenting a market.

● There are many different ways of enhancing a product and increasing its perceived value.

● Every product has a life cycle.

● Services, too, have life cycles.

● In order to prolong product or service life cycles they must be adapted or enhanced to meet the demands of a changing market.

● Successful businesses seize the opportunities change offers.

# Pricing the Product

**6**

If you were approached by someone in the street today and asked what you thought was the right price for a pint of beer, what would you say? And how would that price compare, say, with a glass of mineral water?

A newspaper article suggested that some public houses charge more for a pint of mineral water than they do for a pint of beer. Does this make sense? Perhaps not to you and me, but obviously there are some people who are prepared to pay more for mineral water than for beer.

How about a chocolate bar? What do you think would be the right price for a slab of milk chocolate? Your answer would probably depend on a number of things. It would depend on how much you like chocolate – or more specifically milk chocolate, how long it has been since you had some, how hungry you were, how close it was to a meal time, and so on.

Nor is the price fixed solely on its physical characteristics. Referring back to our pint of beer example, the price you would be prepared to pay not only depends on how thirsty you are, it also depends on where you plan to drink it.

You might well agree to pay more for a drink in a public house than you would for a drink at home. And you would almost certainly pay more to drink in a public house that had a satellite television tuned in to a football game showing your favourite team, especially if they were playing in a crucial cup tie. So what is the right price? Does a right price actually exist?

Similar arguments apply to prices set by the sellers of goods and services. Most manufacturers are prepared to charge less for their products when stocks are high and demand low. In fact many of them hold sales to sell off stock as quickly as possible. In truth, then, there is no such thing as a single, all-embracing 'right price' for anything. If it does exist, it is only what one supplier and one customer agree is right at one particular moment in time.

## Profit

When trying to establish a selling price for any product or service we need to consider the profit we want to make. But what do we mean by profit? Stripped to its bare essentials, profit is that part of income left over when all the expenses of the business have been paid. To put it more bluntly: profit is the lifeblood of the business – the bit that makes it all worthwhile. But there are a number of different ways of identifying profit and they are certainly not the same thing. In the examples that follow a number of different methods have been used to identify a profit margin and arrive at a selling price for the product in question. Although different they have one thing in common: they all set out to ensure that a true profit has been made when all the work has been completed – and paid for. No matter which method you choose to define a profit margin, there has to be one. Without it there would be no money available to reinvest in the assets of the business and, given time, the business would eventually die.

When people talk about profit, one of three things is usually meant:

1. *Gross Margin* – the selling price less all manufacturing costs.

2. *Net Margin* – the gross margin less all overheads.

3. *Net Profit* – the net margin less all financial costs.

## Marginal Cost

We'll begin with marginal cost. What is it exactly? Marginal cost is the cost of making one more when all set-up charges have been recovered. Let's take a book publisher as an example. During the first printing of any title the publisher will want to cover all the costs incurred in its production. There are many of them. Apart from typesetting, photography, repro, printing and paper costs, there are payments to the author and designer, overheads incurred in the editorial and production departments, selling expenses and management charges. These should all be recovered in selling out the first printing – let's say 10,000 copies. But what happens if 10,001 are printed? The final copy will certainly not cost the same as those that preceded it. In fact, the only charges likely to be incurred are for printing and paper, selling expenses and royalty payments to the author. These represent the marginal cost to the publisher after all set-up charges have been recovered – it is the cost of printing one more copy.

In very depressed trading conditions some companies will sell at marginal cost just to cover the costs of production. Charging slightly above marginal cost makes a contribution towards the fixed costs of the business and will keep it ticking over. In the short term doing this can make sense, provided that:

♦ it is seen to be a one-off offer (perhaps a sale to clear stock) and does not set a precedent or upset existing customers who have paid the full price, *or*

♦ the lower price is presented as the normal (or usual) price less a volume/loyalty/introductory discount, *or*

♦ there are no existing hidden discounts for some customers, such as special extended credit terms, which have already been agreed.

The concept of marginal costing can also be useful in the long term when it is related to added value. Any extra or surplus revenue received by pricing above marginal cost is added value, or the contribution made towards recovering the cost of overheads. Properly monitored and controlled, added value can be a great asset, clearly illustrating the true effect of all pricing decisions and making sure that there is enough profit margin in a competitive market place to ensure that all overheads are fully recovered.

In a well-run business it is essential to know:

♦ that gross margins are being earned

♦ what are the marginal costs and break-even levels, and

♦ that all of these are being monitored, analysed and reinforced at frequent intervals.

## Cost-Plus Pricing

Probably the most popular method of pricing a product is what is known as cost-plus. No doubt this is because the concept is much easier to understand than most other methods. What it means is that all costs are calculated as closely as possible, apportioned to one or more products or services, and a suitable profit margin added. It's as simple as that. And for the experienced businessman who keeps a close eye on material prices (including trends) and can make a fairly accurate prediction of any cost fluctuations during the term of a contract (including labour and materials), it can form the basis of reasonably accurate 'off-the-cuff' estimates. But is it close enough? And is it good enough to determine prices simply on the basis of costs and a 'suitable' profit margin? This process might form the basis of a minimum price level, below which we are not prepared to go, but if we learned anything at all from the previous chapter, we must now realise that products are more than the sum of their parts. We also know that many customers do not even recognise seemingly identical products as the same. Despite their physical similarities products are enhanced (or reduced) by many added features that cost very little – perhaps nothing at all. So, if we really are concerned, as we should be, with accurately pricing our products in line with market expectations, we should begin by establishing a pricing policy.

## Pricing Objectives

Every business has objectives: things it wants to achieve within a certain timescale. In textbook terminology these are called corporate objectives. They can be financial (gross profit margin, return on capital etc.), numerical (sales per employee, total sales volume etc.), or size (fastest growing, largest market share etc.). Any objectives relating to price cannot ignore these other corporate objectives.

It doesn't make a lot of sense to adopt a rigid cost-plus pricing policy that totally ignores what is happening elsewhere in the marketplace. And it makes absolutely no sense at all to adopt any rigid pricing policy if the principal corporate objective is to maintain or increase existing market share. In other words, prices should not be set without some reference to already established corporate objectives.

## Pricing Too Low

Many years ago a man tried to sell pound notes (this was long before the introduction of pound coins) outside a railway station, for one penny each. He expected that he would sell out very quickly. In fact he sold very few. Most of the people he approached simply did not believe him. His sales message was not believable. We will learn more about sales and what we must do to make our sales message credible in Chapter 8: Selling the Product. For the time being, though, this highly eccentric example is introduced as a means of making the point that, contrary to popular belief, it is possible to price a product too low.

Companies will often submit low prices to obtain more work, especially when trading conditions are not favourable. When they are particularly bad some will go so far as to offer to undercut any other prices received. In other words the selling price is determined without any reference whatsoever to production costs. And, as a short-term expedient, it can work. In the long run, however, it is necessary – in fact it is essential – to ensure that fixed costs are covered by the volume actually sold and not the volume expected to be sold.

Think of a manufacturer who at the beginning of the year believes that he or she will be able to manufacture and sell 1,000 units of production every week. The fixed costs of the business are worked out, divided by 1,000 units, and allocated equally to each. But what happens if just 800 units are produced? The simplest mental arithmetic will tell you that 20% of the fixed costs will not be recovered. And, if prices are reduced as well, it won't be long before the company is losing quite a lot of money.

There will always be good reasons for giving cheap prices. It may be that you are trying to penetrate a new market where your reputation is unknown and you need a price incentive to make a breakthrough. It could be that you want to make a special promotional offer to get a sluggish market sector moving again. Whatever the reason, you must consider the effect well-publicised price cuts will have on those customers who have already paid your full price. In the interests of price stability it might make sense instead to make concessionary discounts for volume purchases, prompt payment, or even, perhaps, for the time of year the order is placed – a seasonal reduction.

## Impact of Price Reductions

Additionally, it is important to be aware of the impact a price reduction will have on your profitability. For example; if your Gross Margin is 30% and you give a 5% discount (List less 5%), your Gross Margin will fall to 25%. In fact, you will have to sell an additional 20% units at that price just to achieve your original profit forecast. The chart below illustrates the impact of price reductions.

*Impact of price reductions*

| Price Reduction | GROSS PROFIT MARGIN | | | | | | | |
|---|---|---|---|---|---|---|---|---|
| | 5% | 10% | 15% | 20% | 25% | 30% | 35% | 40% |
| | *You must sell this amount to break even* | | | | | | | |
| 1% | 25% | 11.1% | 7.1% | 5.3% | 4.2% | 3.4% | 2.9% | 2.6% |
| 5% | - | 100% | 50% | 33.3% | 25% | 20% | 16.7% | 14.3% |
| 10% | - | - | 200% | 100% | 66.7% | 50% | 40% | 33.3% |
| 15% | - | - | - | 300% | 150% | 100% | 76.8% | 60% |
| 20% | - | - | - | - | 400% | 200% | 133.3% | 100% |
| 25% | - | - | - | - | - | 500% | 250% | 166.7% |

## Pricing Too High

Economists tell us that there is a distinct causal relationship between demand for a product and its price. Some go even further and will plot demand for you on a graph showing how, for any one product, the volume demanded increases as the price decreases, and vice versa. They call it a demand curve. This doesn't work every time, but because it seems to work in most circumstances and the theory has a certain logic to it which most people can understand, it is a very popular concept.

The shape of the curve is also important. An almost horizontal curve means that a small change in price will result in a higher proportionate change in quantity demanded. The product is price sensitive. A vertical curve occurs when a large price reduction is required to obtain a comparatively small change in the quantity demanded. Knowing the shape of a product's demand curve and its price sensitivity is important. If a 10% price reduction increases demand by 50%, profits will probably increase. A 50% price reduction resulting in just a 10% increase in demand is likely to have exactly the opposite effect.

Eventually all pricing decisions come down to objectives. If you are happy with your business and further growth is unimportant to you, you are probably satisfied with things as they are and do not want to tamper with prices in order to increase sales. If, however, you feel that your business is a long way from achieving its full potential and believe that you are not selling enough, either your sales message is wrong, it is not reaching the right people, or your prices need to be adjusted.

## Case Study

*Difficult Pricing Decisions*

*An antique restorer contacted a management consultant requesting help and advice with setting and implementing an effective pricing policy for his business. He was very concerned because he felt that he was subject to intolerable pressures from his customers to keep prices low, yet when he tried to buy in services for his home or business he was constantly being told that the price had gone up since last time. Why weren't other trades affected in the same way as his? He was advised to keep a record of the amount of labour involved in every job he took on and the hourly rate charged. As the consultant expected he was charging considerably less per hour than many less-skilled trades. The consultant quoted many examples of companies in different lines of work who had prospered despite charging more than the going market rate. More than anything, though, the antique restorer was advised not to be defensive about his pricing structure. Buyers of antiques who genuinely look for quality in the products and services they buy have a very different conception of the right price than the average 'bargain hunter'.*

## Pricing for Value

When a pricing decision is made it is important to recognise the association in our minds between price and value. We may sometimes fall victim to buying shoddy merchandise simply because it is being sold at a very cheap price, but in reprimanding ourselves for our stupidity we invariably fall back on that old adage: "You only get what you pay for". And this is true – most of the time. That's why we tend to believe that high prices mean quality and very low prices mean junk. If there is a marked difference between our conception of the product and its selling price we become disturbed and unsettled. We find it difficult to make up our minds to buy. And if you are the one who made the mistake of pricing your product incorrectly so that your prospective customers believe it is either too cheap or too expensive – you could be the one who eventually pays the price.

## The Pricing Paradox

A major manufacturing company decided that one of its most successful products was coming to the end of its life cycle. Three times, the price had been reduced to try and extend its life - but sales continued to fall. Consequently, it was decided that the product should be phased out but the price would be increased to squeeze out the last bit of profitability. The price was increased by 10% - and the sales began to rise! The price was then increased by a further 10% - and the sales rose even further. Fearing that these increased sales would out-strip the limited manufacturing capacity now being applied to this product, the price was increased by a further 10% - sales continued to grow. It was realised that the product was no longer perceived as a 'cheap' product and was now addressing a different segment of the market. Consequently, it was reinstated as a mainline product and to this day makes a considerable contribution to the profitability of the company.

## SUMMARY

● There is no such thing as an all-embracing right price – just what one buyer and one seller agree is right at one moment in time.

● Pricing a product should begin with setting the profit margin required.

● Marginal cost is the cost of making one more when all set-up costs have been recovered.

● Pricing at marginal cost during depressed trading conditions can make sense in the short term.

● Pricing objectives must be compatible with overall corporate objectives.

● Contrary to popular belief, it is possible to price a product too low.

● Selling less than budgeted quantities can mean that the fixed costs of the business are not being recovered.

● Discounts for prompt payment, volume purchased or off-season placement of order can seem more credible to the purchaser than straight price reductions.

● High prices do not necessarily mean that profits are being maximised.

● For most customers there is a definite correlation between price and value.

● Pricing too high or too low can adversely affect product positioning in the marketplace.

# Promoting the Product

7

If we want to sell what we have produced, we have to let potential customers know that we have these products for sale. There are many ways of doing this. We can place an advertisement on television or in a newspaper; we can place a poster on a billboard or on the side of a bus; we can sing about it, shout about it, or even walk around with a sandwich board displaying it. We can even promote our products and services to a global market using the World Wide Web on the Internet. There are many ways. Most of them are called advertising although there are some parts more properly contained within the description, "Sales Promotion". But we will not get hung up on words. We will think simply of promoting our products as effectively as possible and let the categories take care of themselves.

## Advertising

There are few people today who would refute the claim that advertising permeates almost every aspect of our lives. Look around the room you are sitting in now. If it's an office, look at the advertisers' names on calendars, diaries, notepads and deskpads, felt tips and ball points. If you are sitting in your living room, take a look at the newspapers and magazines; flip through the channels on your television or the dial on your radio. Look or listen to some of the advertisements. Then step outside your house and look at the advertisements on buses, tube trains, taxis and railway stations. They are everywhere. And what are they doing? What is their purpose? Well, their principal objective is to get you to buy their products. And they do this by trying to get their name in front of as many potential purchasers as cheaply and effectively as possible.

Advertising alone rarely sells products. (There are exceptions to this which we will discuss later when we come to direct response advertising and point-of-sale.) But by and large, advertising is part of the marketing mix, and it supports or supplements other marketing activities. Advertising creates awareness. For as we know, products move faster off the shelves when they are recognised. In addition, salespeople find it easier to obtain orders from customers who are aware of the company name and feel that they know the products they sell. The main function of advertising is to convey information. It's like a personal message multiplied hundreds, or thousands – perhaps even hundreds of thousands – of times. Price changes, product improvements and new distribution outlets can be notified to customers through advertising. In fact there is one category of advertising, which includes public announcements, financial and tender advertisements, and the like, that has no other objective than to pass on information.

But advertising is very much more than this. For example, one very important facet of advertising is its ability to change attitudes. It is not easy to change deeply entrenched attitudes, but a sustained advertising programme, supported when necessary by endorsements from trustworthy public figures, can reduce prejudice, create fresh attitudes, and help persuade customers that their previous conceptions of a particular product were false.

Advertising, then, helps promote new sales. But it also acts as a reminder to existing customers. When competitors are constantly vying for their attention, it is vital that your customers receive regular reminders of the features and benefits of your products, even if they use them on a regular basis. Brand loyalty although seemingly deeply entrenched should never be taken for granted.

## Advertising Campaigns

When making a plan it is only commonsense to decide, in advance, what it is intended to achieve. And there are few areas in business more in need of detailed planning than advertising campaigns. For if it is not planned properly, advertising can be a terrible waste of money. It used to be considered quite a joke when the advertising manager stood up to say: "I know that half the money I spend on advertising is wasted. The trouble is I don't know which half." But not any more. In these days of tight budgets and strict financial controls, it's simply not good enough to think in terms of wasting money on advertising or anything else for that matter. Detailed advertising campaigns with clearly defined achievable objectives are both prudent and necessary.

The accent on 'achievable' objectives is deliberate. A Rolls-Royce dealer might well hope to sell ten cars through a single, small classified advertisement in the *Wigley Weekly Advertiser.* But he or she is extremely unlikely to achieve it. Response forecasts must make allowance for the media selected, the size of the advertisement, and the frequency of insertion. But they must still be made. If you have ever expressed dissatisfaction with the response received from any advertisement without having previously thought what that response should be – or at least what is acceptable to you – you should look very closely at your advertising budget and ask yourself if it is being spent wisely.

It is of course true that some advertisements are not intended to elicit a response. Perhaps they are part of the information advertising mentioned earlier. But if your advertisements are not intended to get a response, why are you advertising? There must be a reason. You might say that it is to raise the profile of your company in a certain industry. If so, that is your objective. And assuming it is an achievable objective, it should happen. If it does not, you will at least know not to repeat it again later.

## The Media

There are many places in which to insert advertisements these days. The list is almost endless. Whenever a number of people can be persuaded to focus their attention in a certain place, sooner or later an advertisement will appear there. Whether it is a crowd at a football match, a queue at a bus stop, passengers in a taxi, an audience in the cinema, readers of a certain newspaper, viewers of a particular television programme, or surfers of the Net; they all represent potential customers for some product or service.

Broadly speaking, advertising media fall into five broad categories:

### 1 BROADCAST

There was a time, many years ago, when there was no advertising at all on radio or television in the UK. Independent television came first, and later commercial radio. Today with satellite television and a whole range of new specialist radio stations catering for individual tastes in music, the choice is yours. And because it is now possible to select limited geographical coverage, advertising rates have been reduced and there is less wastage for the local advertiser. Today, radio and television advertising is a very important part of many advertising budgets of companies who would once have considered them too expensive.

## 2   PRINTED PUBLICATIONS

Newspapers fall into many different categories: national and regional, daily and weekly, free and paid for. Colour is readily available in many of them but can be quite expensive. New magazines appear with increasing frequency and cover a whole range of specialised interests, pastimes and leisure pursuits. They may be directed towards the trade or consumers, sold on subscription or the news-stands, or they may be distributed free to selected readers, specific trades and occupations or, sometimes, blanket coverage within a specific area.

Most magazines appear in full colour, just a few in black and white. In addition, there are numerous catalogues, directories, reference books, programmes and circulars, most of which will accept advertising of one sort or another. In fact, so wide is the distribution of so many printed publications that advertisers have to be very selective if they want to obtain the best value from their advertising budgets.

## 3   POSTERS

Because of their physical size and frequently dominant position in the High Street, when we think of posters we tend to think of large 24-sheet posters on advertising hoardings. But there are many more. Much smaller in size but every effective are display cards on bus and train carriages. These are also seen inside taxicabs and other places where there is a captive audience. The travelling public will also be aware of outside displays such as those seen on the outside of buses and taxis, or posters placed inside railway and underground stations. In this category we might also include outdoors signs of all kinds – painted, printed and illuminated. However the biggest growth area in poster advertising these days has been at televised sporting events. There are even specialist brokers whose expertise is knowing just where the camera points most often.

## 4   NOVELTY

The catch-all category of novelty advertising covers so many items: pencils, T-shirts, shopping bags, balloons, diaries, calendars, clocks, deskpads, and many more too varied to be listed separately.

## 5   SPONSORSHIP

Advertising sponsorship is a category which has expanded rapidly in recent years and shows little sign of abating. Although we tend to think predominantly of arts and sport sponsorship, it is arguable that advertising placed in a school sports programme or church fete bulletin – both of which are unlikely to receive anything but a very limited response – owe more to sponsorship than anything else. However, for most advertisers sponsorship means wide coverage, and the attraction of large television audiences at most sporting events has considerable appeal. Brand names on footballers' shirts, tennis players' headbands, or motor racing car fins, can be seen by thousands of spectators and millions of television viewers over and over again. No wonder that millions of pounds are spent every year on sports sponsorship.

The appeal of the arts is something quite different and necessarily more subtle. For even in the less formal atmosphere prevalent today, where symphony orchestras have been known to play concerts in other than formal attire, it would still be unacceptable for the conductor or musicians to display brand names on their bodies or their clothing. But in the same way that sports stadia obtain extra revenue from providing hospitality suites where companies can entertain their clients, it is common practice for concert halls and theatres to sell block bookings or boxes for very similar purposes.

## The Message

Memorable advertising slogans sound deceptively simple. So much so that nearly every man and his dog seems to believe that he could create one just as well. Oh that it was as easy as all that! But even the most memorable slogans do not work every time. "You're Never Alone With A Strand" the advertisement claimed when the new cigarette appeared. Most people who saw it remembered it. Unfortunately for the manufacturer, few of them believed it. Or, if they did, they didn't believe it was a good enough reason to change brands.

How then should you present your advertising message? You have chosen the medium to carry it, you may even have a good idea of what you want to say, but how do you get it across? Are there rules that govern the way advertisements should appear? Well in a way yes, in another way no. There are techniques for laying out advertisements and there are dozens of theories explaining why some of them are more effective than others. But if all it took to create a successful advertisement was to follow a few rules of layout and design, everybody would be doing it. Many very sophisticated companies spend thousands of pounds on advertisements that do not work. You can be assured that they do not do it deliberately.

Many years ago a famed advertising pioneer claimed that the secret of success in advertising was to discover a product's 'Unique Selling Point' (USP) and push it for all it's worth. And it seemed to work. Detergents told of their new special ingredient which made whites whiter than white, instant coffees spoke of their unique roasting process which gave their beans a special flavour – and if they told us once they told us a hundred times. It doesn't seem to work quite like that today. Perhaps because we are more sophisticated – possibly because we are a touch more cynical. More likely because we got fed up with the constant repetition. But in a way the advice still holds.

Any advertiser who can find a genuine difference between his or her product and the competition would be foolish not to exploit it. And provided that it is a genuine difference, and that it is a difference that will mean something to the customer, it is bound to attract the right attention when promoted properly. But it has to be a difference that means something. A toilet roll manufacturer once tried to exploit the fact that with his brand of toilet rolls the second roll in a pack of two was individually wrapped for "extra freshness". This must have come as a quite a surprise to many customers, most of whom had never realised before that a toilet roll could go stale. The result was that they didn't believe it, and they didn't buy it. It was a silly idea, soon dropped and forgotten.

When designing or laying out advertisements, one of the biggest mistakes smaller advertisers make is to try to cram too much into a small space. In a way this is only to be expected. Advertising space is not cheap and it must be very tempting to buy a small advertisement and put in as much text as possible. After all, advertisers do not like to feel that they are paying for empty space. In their eyes it's money wasted. But is this really true? Advertisements are there to be noticed and it's amazing how much attention white space attracts – especially on a busy page where everyone else is trying to squeeze in as much information as possible. Look at any page of advertisements today and look closely at the ones you notice first. Chances are that they have an interesting illustration and/or white space around them.

When you think of the thousands of advertisements which fight for our attention every day, it is not difficult to appreciate the importance of a clear and simple uncluttered message. So resist the temptation to be clever. If you get it wrong it will only confuse the customer and your advertisement will be wasted. Remember that we can't all be creative geniuses who think up memorable slogans at the drop of a hat. It's best to think of what you want to say, then say it as simply as possible. Make it believable and avoid ambiguities. Test it out on your friends, family, workmates and customers. Make sure that what they are reading is what you intended to put in. It's so very easy to make mistakes. For example, what does it mean to you when you read: "Buy Two and Get One Free!" Does it mean that you buy two and you will get the third one free? Or does it mean that you buy two and one of these two is free? It makes quite a difference, doesn't it? It could make a very big difference to your profit margin.

What the advertiser should want above all else, is for the customer to remember his or her name. Advertising rarely replaces personal selling entirely – it acts as a complement to it. At some point the sales message in most advertisements must be closed by a personal sales presentation, a sale over the counter, or even an order taken over the telephone. The advertisement is a sales aid and should, above all else, make the advertiser's name memorable. And if you have any difficulty remembering if it was Cinzano or Martini that Leonard Rossiter threw over Joan Collins, you will understand why.

# SUMMARY

- Advertising alone rarely sells products –
  it supports or supplements other marketing
  activities.

- Advertising creates awareness, conveys
  information, helps change attitudes, and
  reminds customers of a product or service.

- Advertising campaigns should be carefully
  planned and work to clearly defined,
  achievable objectives.

- Opportunities for advertising exist in the
  broadcast media, printed publications, indoor
  and outdoor posters and on many novelty items.

- Sponsorship in advertising is rapidly expanding,
  particularly arts and sport sponsorship.

- Creating memorable advertising slogans is much
  more difficult than it sometimes seems.

- Where possible the advertiser should try to find
  a genuine product difference which can be
  exploited through a consistent, sustained
  advertising programme.

- The message should be plain and simple,
  clear and uncluttered.

- White space in and around an advertisement
  is not wasted space.

- What the advertiser wants, above all else, is that
  the customer should remember his or her name.

# Selling the Product

8

It is probably true to say that most marketing textbooks play down the role of the salesperson in the marketing of goods and services. They recognise the sales function as part of the marketing mix but because it is only a part – and not, perhaps, as important a part as most sales people would have it – the sales role gets downgraded. Few business schools teach selling in any meaningful way; most virtually ignore it. The reasons for this are difficult to understand. For although there are a lot of products which on the surface do not require personal selling – maybe they are picked off a shelf or selected from a catalogue page or advertisement – somewhere in the marketing chain someone has to sell something to somebody. Whether it is the advertising agency selling its services to the client, the newspaper or magazine selling advertising space to the agency, or the door-to-door salesperson selling products directly to customers, a sale has to take place at one point or another. To repeat what our sales manager said at the start of Chapter 4: "Nothing happens until somebody sells something."

## The Salesperson

For those who have never been involved in personal selling before, it can appear a daunting prospect. But selling is not always as difficult as we expect it to be. In real life most of us are selling ourselves all the time, without even realising it. And despite popular belief, the fast-talking, wisecracking extrovert does not always make the best salesperson. More often the soft-spoken, sincere individual, selling a product or service which he or she genuinely believes will benefit the customer, is far more effective. But let us assume that you seriously want to become a professional salesperson. How do you go about it? And, more importantly, how do you do it well?

Most of us believe that salespeople are born and not made and, to a certain extent, this is true. Some do seem to have an intuitive feel for understanding the needs of others, and for recognising key points in the process of persuasion which turn moments of reflection into moments of decision. But no salesperson is ever so good that he or she could not benefit from sales training at some point in his or her career. In that sense then, good salespeople are, "born – and then made". And when it comes to those who do not see themselves as salespeople, although they are responsible for the sales function – small company owners or managers for example – they can improve their sales effectiveness considerably by learning and applying basic selling philosophies.

## Personal Selling

But why bother with salespeople at all, you might ask? If my work is good enough, satisfied customers will become my salesforce. They will recommend my work and new customers will come to me automatically. There is some truth in this. Although it is doubtful that the world will beat a pathway to your door if you build a better mousetrap, there are many examples of individuals and even companies that seem to prosper without any sales representation at all. As an example, consider a small workshop owned and operated by a group of specialist craftsmen and women who have no salesforce yet seem to have a never-ending flow of customers anxious to buy their products.

How do they do it? Well, for a start it's very unlikely that they do not have a salesforce. More likely the principals are salesmen and women without even realising it. They are handling objections, answering queries, closing the sale and following up after the work is completed – everything a good salesperson would do as a matter of course. So many successful salespeople begin their presentation claiming that they are not salespeople at all. And, despite their more obvious successes, they do actually believe it. That is because we all seem to have a very biased picture of what a good salesperson actually does.

## Where to Start

The really good salesman or woman begins by building up his or her inner strengths, then looks outside to develop the technical skills which will improve performance and help increase sales. Let's start with building up the inner strengths. What exactly does this mean? What it means is building up personal self-esteem to cope with the setbacks and rejections personal selling inevitably brings.

There are two things which cause more failures in selling than anything else. The first is lack of self-confidence and the second is fear of rejection. Successful salespeople learn to overcome the one and to cope with the other. You can overcome your lack of self-confidence by developing a positive mental attitude. Instead of concentrating on what has gone wrong, we can direct our thoughts to what has gone right. One suggestion might be to develop a victory list where you record all your sales successes. Everyone deserves a pat on the back occasionally and there is no reason why you can't generate it for yourself if nobody else does it for you.

The most common cause of failure in selling comes from fear of rejection. We all have it. We're born with it. It's part of our makeup. But some find it easier to cope with than others. For the salesperson it is imperative that he or she learns to cope with it. Four out of five attempts to close the sale will result in a negative response. The successful salesperson has to learn that rejections are not personal, and that they are frequently followed by sales success.

## When to Close

Choosing the right moment to close the sale is one of the most difficult parts of the selling process. Asking for the order is almost like inviting rejection and no one wants that. In fact some less successful salespeople will do anything to avoid it, often talking far beyond the point where the sales interview should have been concluded. No wonder then that the biggest complaint buyers make about sales people is that they talk too much.

It is much easier to close a sale if the right preparations are made in the first place. There was a time when salespeople were told that almost half the sales interview should be devoted to closing the sale. Times have changed and the new model of selling has changed with it. Instead of boring the buyer to death with endless repetitions of different closing techniques, modern salesmen and women are taught to spend 40% of their time building an atmosphere of trust with their customers, 30% discovering the customer's needs, 20% making the presentation, and just 10% closing the sale. When 90% of the sales interview has been handled effectively, the close becomes instinctive – almost second nature. In the process, of course, there will be many objections. These are inevitable and to be encouraged. A successful sale cannot be made without them. But it has to be remembered that objections are not rejections. Learning to cope with them is a most important part of the salesperson's function.

## The Buying Process

The big difference between a good salesperson and a great salesperson is that the latter probably has a better understanding of why customers actually buy. For it's a strange fact that although we, as consumers, recognise our need for new products or services, most of us have an in-built resistance to being sold to. Perhaps it's something to do with a deep-seated desire to believe that our decisions are made independently; that we are not being persuaded into anything. But whatever the reason, it's there.

The vast majority of buying decisions are based on emotion. We may use logic and reason to justify our decisions but they are rarely the original cause. We just feel that it is right to buy that particular product. That is why a successful salesperson will always remember that he or she is not selling a product, but satisfaction. The product or service is sold not on price, but value for money – not on features, but benefits.

---

## Case Study

*An industrial salesman working for a major aggregate company, was asked what he sold, and who he sold it to. His answer was that he sold tarmac to construction contractors. When asked why customers bought from him rather than his competitors, he said his company always delivered on time and within the client's specification.*

*Most of his customers' projects were taken on penalty clauses and they were on call 24 hours a day. If deliveries were late, or outside specification, that customer's life could be made a misery. That discussion helped the salesman to understand that what he was REALLY selling was peace of mind to individuals who were under immense pressure.*

*Salespeople who analyse what they are really selling achieve more sales and develop better relationships with their customers.*

---

## The Hidden Objection

No salesperson is successful every time. For some customers it really is the wrong product, the wrong time, or the wrong price – perhaps even a combination of all three. But some sales are lost simply because the salesperson never gets to hear of the hidden objection.

During any sales presentation the prospect is certain to offer objections. In most cases he or she will be looking for reassurance. If he or she claims to be worried that you may not be able to deliver on time, this may be a signal that a more concrete guarantee is required that your delivery promises will be kept. If, on the other hand, your prospect has heard from a disgruntled customer that your quality is suspect, there may be an understandable reluctance to tell you this. And if it worries the prospect enough you may be given another reason altogether as to why the order is not being placed with you. "The price is too high" or "I can't afford it" are two of the favourite reasons given for not placing an order.

These objections are easy to say without causing offence and difficult to challenge. Many salespeople respond by offering to reduce the price –

assuming that they have the authority to do so. And if the price reduction is sufficient to cancel the worry of the hidden objection, it can work. But it is not always the answer. Before making this move it would make sense to ask if price is the only problem. And if it really is nothing more than an excuse to hide a hidden objection, it is amazing how often this simple question will reveal it. In a way it's as though the salesperson is giving the prospect an excuse for saying something that might otherwise cause offence.

A good salesman or woman will always be on the alert for the hidden objection and will allow the prospect every opportunity to voice it.

## On-going Relationships

It has been said that the difference between the salesman and the confidence trickster is that the salesman is usually welcomed back. And, in the process of selling, many salesmen and women do become friends with their customers. It is all part of building an on-going relationship.

The amount of contact any salesperson has with his or her customers will vary with the nature of the business. Someone selling print is likely to make many more calls on the same customer than someone selling life assurance. A print buyer will almost certainly place more orders than the purchaser of life assurance policies. But even someone selling very infrequent purchases will want to maintain some contact, even if it consists of nothing more than a Christmas card and the occasional telephone call. You never know when new business may be around the corner or a recommendation is there simply for the asking. Investing in an on-going relationship benefits both buyer and seller.

## Sales Opportunities

In every business it is almost always true that the greatest source of new business comes from existing customers. Satisfied customers return time and time again and when they are not buying, they are often making recommendations. Some of these recommendations will be made without any prompting at all. It can be surprising how often satisfied customers will act as surrogate salesmen and women for those who have given good service, and even give written recommendations. And if it is not done without prompting the good salesperson will always ask satisfied customers if they know of anyone else who might benefit from their products or services. Introductions are always more effective than cold calls.

## Sales Success

The difference between failure and success in selling, as with so many other things in life, is closer than most of us think. A man once said that a horse that regularly wins by a nose invariably wins ten times the prize money of the horse that came second. But it's not ten times faster – it's only a nose faster. And that can be the difference between failure and success. Being just marginally better than your competitors can have a dramatic effect upon your results.

If you really want to be a successful salesperson you have to be aware of certain rules. You need to:

◆ Set clear goals and keep them constantly in view.
   Remember, you can't hit a target you cannot see.

◆ Commit yourself to excellence and make a decision to
   improve yourself and your skills as much as you can.

◆ Accept 100% responsibility for all that you do, and do not
   blame lost sales on others.

◆ Care about your customers – care passionately for them.

◆ Learn to use time wisely and do not procrastinate.

◆ Sell to your customers as you would like to be sold to.

◆ And, most of all, remember that customers do not buy products
   or services. They buy solutions.

# SUMMARY

- At some point in the marketing chain someone has to sell something to some body.

- Fast-talking, wisecracking extroverts do not always make the best salespeople.

- Soft-spoken, sincere salesmen and women, selling products they believe in, often achieve the best results.

- Lack of self-confidence and fear of rejection are the major causes of failure in selling.

- Good salespeople bolster their confidence with a positive mental attitude.

- Good salespeople progress by developing the technical skills that improve performance and increase sales.

- Successful salespeople actually help their customers to buy.

- Knowing how and when to close a sale is extremely important.

- The most successful salespeople are always on the alert for the hidden objection.

- Recommendations from satisfied customers are the best sales aids.

- Success comes from treating people the way you like to be treated.

- Customers do not buy products or services – they buy solutions.

- If you really care for your customers – it will show.

# Distributing the Product

9

Probably the most consistent complaint made by marketing practitioners is that they are frequently mistaken for salespeople. In a way this is understandable. So much of the marketing function is concerned with selling the product and, let's be honest about it, the prime responsibility of the marketing department is to move merchandise off the shelves. But, as we know, there's much more to marketing than sales alone. We have already considered pricing, promoting and selling the product. We will now concentrate our attention on distributing the product.

## Choosing the Right Channel

If you were the manufacturer of puncture repair kits for bicycle tyres, would you try to sell them through a supermarket? Unlikely. A hardware store? Possibly. A cycle shop? Most definitely. By their very nature, some products are sold in very specific places. But these places do not always remain the same. Think of a petrol station. Ten years ago would you have thought that you could buy sandwiches from a petrol station? Today many people do. They also purchase confectionery, music cassettes, compact discs, magazines, newspapers, flowers, watering cans, and even Christmas trees. Many petrol stations today are mini-supermarkets. How times change!

In this context a petrol station can be called a marketing channel. Deciding where you are going to sell your product is called channel management. At first it seems to be quite simple. Decide where you think your product will sell best, then go for it. Yet when you stop to consider the changes that have taken place in retailing over the last few years – of which petrol stations are just one example – you soon begin to appreciate the dynamics of channel management, and the demands made on marketing people to keep abreast of them.

It is almost a cliché to say it but manufacturers, importers and agents need to be constantly alert to the changes taking place in distribution and the opportunities and threats they represent to many existing successful companies.

## Channel Coverage

Just for a minute let us suppose that you really are the manufacturer of puncture repair kits for bicycles mentioned above. Would you confine your distribution simply to cycle shops? You might. But then one day you would notice that one of your customers has gone out of business and you no longer have any coverage within that particular town. What would you do? Well, you could hope that someone else will realise the opportunity this gap in the market now creates and, as a result, open another cycle shop to replace the one that has closed. That's one solution. On the other hand you could hope that those cycle owners requiring puncture repair kits would go to the next town where your distributor there has good stocks of your product and could use the extra business. Or, if you preferred more direct action, you could approach another business in the town – possibly a hardware store – point out how many of your puncture repair kits the failed cycle shop sold, and suggest that the hardware store should take over the stocking of your product in the town.

Who knows, you might find that your new distributor is more successful than the last. For in addition to selling to cycle owners in the town, he or she might decide to sell them to owners of other inflatable products. And all of a sudden, almost by accident, you have discovered a new market.

This is, of course, a very simplistic and over-simplified case study, but from it you might well draw the conclusion that you should sell your product in as many places as possible, and to as many outlets as possible. And some manufacturers do this. Others look to selective distribution where only those considered likely to do a good job for the product are given the necessary approval. This is particularly important if the product's image is likely to suffer if sold in the wrong place. You wouldn't, for example, want to sell an exclusive brand of ladies' perfume in a fish and chip shop. In fact, for a product like this you might prefer to offer your entire distribution to one retail chain, or even grant exclusive sales rights to one wholesaler in one particular area. (This area, by the way, could be a whole country. It could even be a continent.)

Before making such a major decision you will want to know quite a lot about your potential distributor. You will want to know all you can about his or her reputation. You will also need some reassurance about his or her representation. What you are looking for is someone who can push your product through the channel.

The distributor, on the other hand, will be looking at the proposed agreement from another perspective completely. Before agreeing to your terms the distributor will want to know what support you are prepared to offer to pull your products through the channel. For example, what are your plans for advertising and promotion? What incentives will you offer to encourage those who actually sell the product? What will you do to support your distributor?

## Specialist Distributors

Amongst distributors there are many specialists. Some of these have great sales coverage in certain areas. Others have specialist knowledge and contacts for selling your type of product. And if what you have to offer interests them and shows great sales potential, they will almost certainly take it on and help promote it.

When entering a distribution agreement, especially where exclusivity is on offer, it is important to make sure that the distributor makes a commitment to move agreed volumes of merchandise within agreed timescales. The agreement should also clearly specify that failure to meet agreed sales targets will result in the loss of exclusivity.

One thing that needs to be particularly stressed is that in agreements between manufacturers and distributors, any matters relating to the agreement must always be conveyed in writing. This is most important where there has been a breach of the agreement. The point is: do something about it now. Do not wait, hoping that it will resolve itself in time. For if you do not act immediately you may be setting up an alternative deal by default. If it has been specified that the exclusive nature of the agreement is conditional on a certain amount of merchandise being moved within a certain period and a lesser amount has been sold, you should write to the distributor pointing out that whilst you recognise the shortfall and are prepared to tolerate it in this instance, this in no way changes the contractual terms of your agreement.

Channel management is a very important part of the marketing function. It is also a fast-moving and fast-changing business area in which manufacturers, importers and agents should recognise the changes as they happen and try to anticipate the effects they are likely to have on other parts of the marketing chain.

## Transportation

It wasn't so very long ago that the majority of goods distributed in the UK were transported by rail. Around that time it would also have been the case that consignments from overseas would arrive almost exclusively on board ship. Not any longer. Some goods still travel by rail and most goods from overseas still reach the UK on a ship. But the balance has changed considerably; more in one case than the other. Transporting goods by air is still very expensive and only the lightest and most urgent consignments are sent that way. But there are certainly more of them. And as for goods transported inside the UK, rail carriers have now given way almost entirely to road hauliers.

The big advantage of road transportation, of course, is door-to-door collection and delivery. Several specialist carriers offer a variety of delivery options to anywhere in mainland UK, as well as bulk rates for daily collection. These rates can be surprisingly low. How long they can be sustained, however, is quite a different matter. Environmental considerations are already causing petrol prices and road taxes to rise faster than inflation, and motorway tolls cannot be far away, thus increasing road transportation costs even further.

Some experts are in fact suggesting that a swing back from road to rail is already underway. True or not, it is quite certain that environmental pressures, parking restrictions in inner cities, longer and longer delays caused by increased traffic congestion, and other considerations will bring further changes in the way manufacturers and wholesalers distribute their products to retailers in the High Street.

## Retail Outlets

Of all the changes that have taken place in the UK during the last generation or so, none has been more dramatic than the way we go about our shopping. Thirty or forty years ago there were few supermarkets, most women shopped on a daily basis, and all transactions were recorded on a cash register, without a till roll, in pounds, shillings and pence (and halfpennies and farthings). The difference with today is just about equivalent to the comparison between switching on a computer and sharpening the nib on a quill pen.

But we do not have to go anywhere near as far back as that to appreciate the rate of change that has taken place in the High Street. Even in the last 10 years an amazing number of well-known names have completely disappeared as new, fast-moving competitors have moved in to take their business. Some of these competitors have taken customers to new locations: out-of-town shopping centres, DIY superstores, hypermarkets and the like. Many department stores too have gone. And those that survive have largely become stores-within-stores as smaller retail companies have taken over much of their floor space. The implications for those selling their products through these outlets can be very serious.

---

## Case Study

*In the 1960s a manufacturer of blue jeans had a policy of giving the same discount to all retail customers no matter what level of purchases they made. His products were in demand everywhere and he knew that his simple discount policy would enable his many small rural customers to compete on equal terms with the larger city stores. What he was doing was ensuring the loyalty of the 80% of his customers who made up 20% of his sales. But as blue jeans became more popular and competitors offering volume discounts came into the market, his sales went into decline. His smaller rural customers were in areas of low growth or even declining population, whereas the larger city stores were expanding rapidly. Within ten years the manufacturer had disappeared, taken over by one of his competitors. It was not simply his pricing policy that cost him his business. It was failing to understand the importance of managing his distribution channels.*

## Direct-to-User

Considering the number of mail-order catalogues that land on the average householder's doorstep every year, it would seem that catalogue companies are flourishing. And they are – most of them. Those that have moved into the High Street and offer brand-named goods at discounted prices are doing well. So too are the smaller, specialist catalogue companies who have identified a definite market sector, and meet the needs of their customers by bringing the products they require to their door, rather than leaving them to search up and down the High Street for what they want.

The larger catalogue companies have tended to lose market share in recent years. Traditionally their markets consisted of those who wanted to purchase items on credit by making small, regular weekly payments. Nowadays their appeal is much more to those who want to find things quickly and have little time to look around the shops.

Shopping from home may be one of the biggest growth areas in the next few years. With both husbands and wives working full time in many households, families want their spare time to be leisure time. One supermarket chain is already trying to capitalise on this by accepting phoned, faxed and home computer generated orders and delivering them, for a fee, direct to the shopper. Although confirmed to a few selected areas at the moment, take up by the elderly and by working mothers, in particular, suggests that it may well become an established part of future shopping patterns.

Telephone selling is on the increase, as is direct response from television advertising. Other methods of selling directly to the end user include direct mail, magazine and newspaper coupon offers, house parties, vending machines and exhibitions, to name just a few. The Internet is the newest and one of the fastest growing. All these affect the way goods are sold and distributed. No doubt others will appear in the future, offering new sales opportunities to marketing managers with vision and imagination.

One of these will almost certainly be database marketing, where companies that at one time thought they were just selling goods to customers are now aware that they provide a service to named individuals. Thanks to the computer, it is now possible for these companies to contact their customers with special offers and promotions as often as they wish. Products which they once sold over the counter may now be distributed by mail or even delivered directly from the manufacturer, agent or importer.

## SUMMARY

- Some products need to be sold in very specific places or channels.

- Deciding where to sell your product is called channel management.

- Channels are not static and the products they distribute can change.

- Marketing-oriented companies are constantly alert to the opportunities and threats offered by changes in distribution.

- It is not always possible or wise to sell your products in as many places as possible. The product's image can suffer if it is sold in the wrong place.

- Distribution coverage for any product may be intensive, selective or exclusive.

- The terms of an exclusive distribution agreement must be adhered to and the consequences of any deviation confirmed in writing.

- Many traditional High Street shoppers now buy in quantity from out-of-town locations.

- Department stores are becoming more stores-within-stores.

- Shopping from home is adding new life to some catalogue companies.

- Telephone selling, television direct response and other new direct-to-user sales methods are bringing changes in distribution.

- Database marketing will almost certainly create further changes in channel management.

# 10

# Negotiating

Marketing is a two-way street along which information should be constantly flowing in both directions. To appreciate this you have only to observe how marketing focused companies put so much effort into obtaining feedback from their customers. We call this market research. But there is another two-way process in which marketing is clearly involved, and that is buying and selling. Marketing practitioners buy advertising space or printed material, then use these media to sell their products. This process of buying and selling involves negotiations which will influence the ultimate profitability.

Everyone in the organisation is negotiating, either internally or externally. Some external negotiators can gain or lose the equivalent of a whole year's salary in one negotiation. That is why this marketing book has a whole chapter devoted to the subject.

## Reaching Agreement

If you look back far enough you will see that people have been negotiating with each other since the beginning of time. It is part of our makeup. The reason for this is quite simple; the potential for negotiation exists in any place and at any time whenever and wherever people buy and sell. Contrary to popular belief though, negotiation is not a competition, and the best negotiators are not necessarily hard, ruthless individuals. Negotiation is really nothing more than a process through which different parties commit themselves to use their best endeavours in trying to reach an agreement.

Skilful negotiators try to bring reality into a situation where one, or both parties, may have unrealistic aspirations. As we know, it doesn't always succeed and, when it doesn't, deadlock is the inevitable result. What we have to remember is that negotiation is one area of business life where both parties really can help each other at little or no cost to themselves. There is always something that one party can concede which costs them very little – but is very valuable to the other party – and vice versa. Skilful negotiators identify these concessions at the planning stage.

## Mutual Satisfaction

It has been said that a key trait of successful negotiators is the ability to have – and demonstrate – a genuine concern for the satisfaction of the other party. This may sound like a paradox, but it is true. None of us like to negotiate with someone who seems oblivious to, and uncaring about, our needs. We are much more likely to reach agreement with someone who seems to care about the satisfaction which get from the negotiation. And it is important to recognise that we are negotiating each other's satisfaction.

Money, terms and conditions, rights and responsibilities are all involved – but they are merely elements of that satisfaction. Research through negotiation exercises has proved that one negotiator can leave a negotiation with an excellent monetary deal, but very low satisfaction, because of the way the negotiation was conducted. Do you think this happens in real life negotiations? Of course it does. Satisfaction is a function of what the negotiator aspires to achieve, and what they actually achieve. Good negotiators try to leave the other party with a high satisfaction level. This can be done in two ways: a) give them more of what they want, or b) lower their perception of what they are likely to receive. Either way, their satisfaction level will increase.

Obviously, the skilful negotiator focuses on the latter course of action. Successful negotiators know that by lowering the other party's aspirations of what they *might* achieve, they will raise their satisfaction in what they *do* achieve.

Success has been achieved when both parties are satisfied with the outcome, happy to fulfil their obligations and would be willing to do business together again. This may seem like an ideal, but it is what skilful negotiators achieve over and over again. In this chapter we will explain how.

## Traits of a Successful Negotiator

There are a number of qualities which go towards making a successful negotiator. Some of them come at birth – although they can always be improved upon with practice and hard work. Others can be acquired through training. Amongst the former are a general practical intelligence, an ability to think clearly under stress, good verbal skills, and an ability to tolerate (although not accept) ambiguity and uncertainty. The latter include good product knowledge, personal integrity, an ability to recognise and exploit power, and excellent planning skills, but most of all, to be consistently successful, a negotiator has to feel confident of his or her ability and possess a strong inner desire to succeed.

---

### Case Study

*A presentation on negotiation was given to a group of managing directors at a networking club. One of them mentioned that he was going to the USA the following week to negotiate the sale of his business. He hadn't previously given any thought to team negotiation.*

*On reflection, he felt that there would be at least three people negotiating on behalf of the purchaser, whereas he would be on his own. Suddenly, he was horrified at the thought of the weakness of his own position in this, the most important negotiation of his life.*

*With this new knowledge, the other group members devoted the rest of the afternoon to helping him plan his negotiation, and one even volunteered to accompany him on the trip. They decided that he would lead the negotiation and the volunteer would act as note-taker and observer.*

*After producing a detailed plan and raising the targets, they left full of confidence and eagerly looking forward to the negotiation. The outcome was a selling price and terms and conditions far in excess of what the managing director had hoped for only one week earlier, and he was able to give a handsome reward to the colleague who accompanied him.*

*This episode emphasised to the whole group the importance of planning, teamwork, identifying roles and setting high targets in negotiation.*

---

## Aspiration and Achievement

An aspiration is a personal commitment which negotiators make to themselves. Everyone sets themselves goals, even though sometimes they may be unaware that they are doing so. And those with higher aspirations will reach higher goals. When people expect and want less, they are usually satisfied with less. It should come as no surprise, therefore, that in negotiations between those of equal power the one who gains most is the one with higher aspirations.

When people state what they *hope* to achieve from a negotiation, that is not an aspiration. It is little more than a dream, and if they don't achieve it, it won't hurt too much. When they state what they *intend* to achieve, that is an aspiration. Then if they don't achieve it, it will be a blow to their ego. Someone who states that they hope to sell their house for £150,000, will probably be happy with £140,000. Someone who states that they intend to get at least £150,000 for their house will construct their thoughts, plans and actions in a way which gives them a much better chance of achieving it. We will explain how to apply this in the section headed 'Setting Targets'.

Consequently, the aspiration is the driving force which leads negotiators to want and achieve more.

## Planning and Preparation

A major part of any negotiation takes place long before any negotiations begin, in the planning that precedes it. It has been claimed that the most important skill of any good negotiator is planning ability. Yet it is amazing how many quite senior business people go into major negotiations with little or no planning at all. What sort of plans should be made in advance of a negotiation?

**Prepare an agenda** – Well first and foremost an agenda has to be prepared. It is much too easy to be blown off course if you are not prepared. You then come away dissatisfied because a number of the points which you thought were important have not been covered. An agenda will help you to stay in control of the negotiation.

**Decide roles** – If you are part of a negotiating team it is vital to decide in advance which roles are going to be adopted by each team member. From popular television films we are all familiar with the 'hard man–soft man' approach where one member of a team asks the hard or difficult questions whilst the other investigates more sympathetically. But there are other more important negotiating roles which many negotiating teams overlook. One person should be designated to 'lead' the negotiation. This avoids the likelihood of being interrupted by your own team member at a crucial point.

Another should be designated to take notes and record what happens. It is wasteful for every member of the team to be making notes. A third might do nothing more than listen and observe. This is a critical role because that person will see and hear things that the others have overlooked. If it is necessary to involve a technical or legal member in your negotiating team, this is an excellent role for them.

It is physically impossible for one person simultaneously to speak, listen, make notes and observe effectively. When the importance of the outcome justifies it, you should negotiate as a team, ensuring that each team member knows clearly what their role is in the negotiation.

**Assess your power** – Before any negotiating takes place, it makes sense to research your power. In a desire for a successful outcome, it is very common to under estimate your own power and over estimate the power of the other party. Power, though, is always relative. It may be real or apparent and it exists only to the extent that it is recognised and accepted by the other party. A lot of it is in the mind, but research has shown that those who believe they have less power start to under estimate their capability, even in the face of evidence to the contrary. Those who really believe they do have power always negotiate from a position of strength.

**If you fail to plan – you are planning to fail**

◆ planning takes time – but planning for negotiation is the best time investment you can make in business

◆ develop a standard format – it takes the hard work out of planning

◆ in your standard format, address the following:

| | |
|---|---|
| OBJECTIVES | What are we trying to achieve? |
| STRATEGIC GOALS | Why do we need it? |
| TARGETS | What do we aspire to and how much room do we have for manoeuvre? |
| HISTORY | How good a client are they to us? How good a supplier are we to them? |
| POWER | What are our areas of power? What are their areas of power? How do they perceive our power? |
| STRUCTURE | What should be on the agenda? What are the four key issues? |
| POSITIONS | What is our estimate of THEIR targets/ needs / essentials |
| CONCESSIONS | What do we WANT? What could we GIVE? |
| ASSUMPTIONS | What are the facts? What are the assumptions? |
| RECONNAISSANCE | What information can we get before the negotiation – who can get it for us? |
| ROLES | Who should lead the negotiation? Who else should be there? What should their prime roles be? |

## Setting Targets

When going into a negotiation it is important to set targets for what you want to achieve. It will help if you identify the best you think you could hope for, what you really intend to gain (your aspiration), and decide well in advance what your fall back position will be.

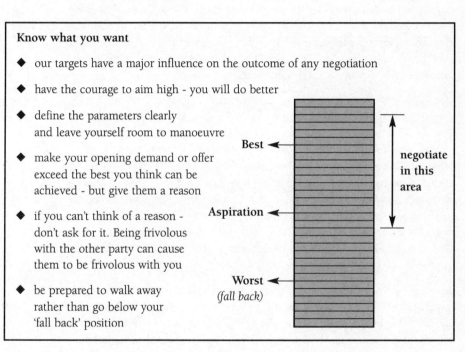

**Know what you want**

◆ our targets have a major influence on the outcome of any negotiation

◆ have the courage to aim high - you will do better

◆ define the parameters clearly and leave yourself room to manoeuvre

◆ make your opening demand or offer exceed the best you think can be achieved - but give them a reason

◆ if you can't think of a reason - don't ask for it. Being frivolous with the other party can cause them to be frivolous with you

◆ be prepared to walk away rather than go below your 'fall back' position

Best

Aspiration

Worst
*(fall back)*

negotiate in this area

In any venture the most reliable path to success lies in knowing what you want to achieve and how you intend to go about it. In negotiation it helps to set targets high. The most successful negotiators are those who make high initial demands and concede as little as possible, as slowly as possible. This is because the initial demand has a major impact on the aspirations of the other party. However, they are always able to give reasons for the demands they are making. The negotiator who makes unjustified demands appears frivolous – and usually causes the other party to become frivolous, leading to deadlock.

## Concessions

During any negotiation some compromise is necessary if deadlock is to be avoided. This usually involves making concessions – and the perceived value of the concession is the key issue. There are many dangers inherent in concession making. Many negotiators review an apparently successful negotiation only to find that they have thrown away the profit in making concessions. Another danger is conceding so readily that they devalue the concession, lowering the satisfaction of the other party and making them feel that they should have asked for more. The harder you make them fight for any concession – the more they will value and appreciate it.

Consequently, we should never go into a major negotiation without having prepared a concession list showing exactly what we can concede and what we might ask for in return. Negotiators shouldn't view a concession as a failure. It can be the one small thing that makes your whole proposal acceptable. However, it is important to have estimated the cost (to you) and the value (to them) of the concessions when preparing your concession list. When seeking major concessions it is always wise to ask for more than you expect to receive – giving yourself room to manoeuvre and the other party the opportunity to negotiate the concession. Likewise, when making a major concession, it is always wise to ask for something in return. The best time to obtain a concession is when you are conceding one.

**Emotion** – There are no rules to negotiating and nothing to say that a negotiator has to act in logical manner. Sometimes it pays to pretend to be unreasonable or irrational. It puts the other side off balance. But you must always remain in control of your feelings. The negotiator who becomes emotional becomes weaker in that negotiation. Negotiators who remain in control are able to vary their style of behaviour in a disciplined fashion. Negotiations can be tense and intimidating, and it is easy to see why the inexperienced can lose control and react angrily. It should be remembered that self discipline builds confidence and confidence minimises the fear of failure.

**Standard Format** – Planning takes time, and time is the most precious and elusive resource of any business person. But planning for negotiation is the best time investment anyone can make in their business. We can take some of the hard work out of planning by developing a standard format, in other words listing and asking ourselves the same questions before every negotiation. An example of a standard format is shown on page 80. Develop your own standard format, circulate it to every one in your team soliciting their help (people really do like to be involved) and your planning will be less time consuming and more effective. The old adage is very true: if you fail to plan – you are planning to fail.

## Phases of a Negotiation

There are four different phases: *Exploratory,* where both sides are trying to sound each other out before making a commitment; *Co-operative,* where both sides acknowledge a desire to reach an agreement acceptable to both sides; *Competitive,* where both sides are trying to obtain as much advantage over the other as possible; and *Deadlock.*

These phases occur in all negotiations and not necessarily in that order. Effective negotiators try to stay in control of the negotiation by controlling the phases. They can be competitive, then co-operative, then exploratory, then back to another phase. The party in control will ensure that the negotiation is in the phase they want – when they want it. They may even risk trial deadlocks. This is an effective way to find out how serious the other party is about a particular point, as suggested earlier, deadlocks can be broken. The major cause of most deadlock situations is personal ego, and if you really want to break a deadlock you usually have to be prepared to sacrifice your ego – practise humility. This is not losing face. It is having the courage and humility, to stay in control. If you can to see how this works in practical terms, it may pay you to practise in a less important negotiation by forcing a deadlock and observing how it is resolved. Be prepared to walk away (metaphorically speaking) and walk back again, then change to another phase.

Negotiation is not a complex activity. It requires planning, and the more you know about the other party, the more effective you will be. It requires confidence, and the better planned you are the greater your confidence will be. It requires concern, concern that the other party should be happy with the final outcome. In fact, the golden rule of negotiation is the golden rule of life: "negotiate with others as you would have them negotiate with you". If you do that, you will have far more successes than failures.

# SUMMARY

- The potential for negotiation exists whenever people buy and sell.

- Skilful negotiators bring reality into a situation where one or both parties may have unrealistic aspirations.

- Negotiation is one area of business life where both sides can help each other at little or no cost to themselves.

- Successful negotiators have, and demonstrate, a genuine concern for the satisfaction of the other party.

- We must lower the aspirations of the other party.

- Success is when both parties are satisfied with the outcome, happy to fulfil their obligations and do business together again.

- Those who aim higher will do better.

- An aspiration is what we INTEND to achieve – not what we HOPE to achieve.

- An important skill of any good negotiator is planning ability.

- Those who believe they have power always negotiate from strength.

- Trade concessions – always ask for something in return.

- The negotiator who becomes emotional becomes weaker in that negotiation.

- Stay in control of the phases of the negotiation.

- Be prepared to risk deadlock – walk away, then walk back again.

- Negotiate with others as you would have them negotiate with you.

# Direct Marketing

**11**

Direct marketing is completely different from most other forms of marketing activities. Although it is sometimes used to complement, or supplement, other selling techniques such as advertising and public relations, direct marketing should be able to stand alone.

The objectives are very simple and straightforward. Direct marketing is used as a means to obtain a response, and sometimes to go through the complete sales message – attracting attention, arousing interest, creating desire and stimulating the potential customer into immediate action, to buy the product or service on offer.

In recent years, the growth of direct marketing has been considerable, and is set to continue expanding as a means for selling products and services for many more years to come. Direct response advertising in printed media such as magazines and newspapers has always been with us, and more recently there has been a huge increase in direct response television advertising, with the development of cable and satellite television.

The era of catalogue shopping via the television set in our homes is still in its infancy. It is predicted that over the next few years, we will be able to purchase virtually any item we require simply by pressing buttons on a key pad. We can already purchase goods via some of the specialist 'shopping channels' without the need to even 'phone through our orders. With banks, the Post Office, supermarkets and suppliers linking up together, the money is simply transferred from the customer's account to that of the seller, and the item/s delivered.

Running parallel to this development is that of e-mail and the Internet. This again works along the lines of shopping via the television, but this time it opens up the entire world as a shop window for your products and services.

Although there is still a way to go to ensure total security in the area of financial transactions, the Net is going to be the future for low cost, direct selling.

These new developments in technological advancement add further impetus to direct response advertising. They allow the customer to see the products in use and therefore respond more positively to the sales message. The ability to be able to pay by credit card and take delivery without leaving the home or office is a major boost to their increasing popularity.

Direct mail, once the Cinderella of the advertising profession, has increased in importance over recent years. With costs rising all the time, and advertisers anxious to reduce wastage, the value of sales targeting has spurred many to look more closely at a method of advertising to precisely those potential customers likely to be interested in the product or services on offer.

It is true to say that direct mail has also been used for blanket coverage – where those not interested in the sales message have reacted in a negative way, calling it 'junk mail', a label which unfortunately has stuck.

With so many mailing lists on offer by companies, there is no reason why this should be so. Any sales message which arouses interest and concern in the recipient could never be called junk, whether it is offering loans for credit risk customers, promoting sales of encyclopedias to university students or inviting contributions for famine relief in Africa.

## The List

One of the secrets of success in direct mail advertising is finding the right list. In today's business environment there are literally thousands of lists available – from active and speculative investors, to labour-saving appliance buyers, and from vacuum cleaner repairers to tool manufacturers and suppliers. Agencies exist to provide lists on paper, gummed labels, computer discs and even downloaded from the Internet. They may be sorted in many ways which are favourable to obtaining large discounts on postage e.g. post codes, geographical areas etc. They may even be personally addressed by name and/or designation – 'Mr. Charles Smith, Managing Director'.

It is a good idea to obtain duplicate lists to allow for follow-up mailings, and sometimes, print-outs may be provided, for a small additional charge, which can include even more detail such as telephone numbers, fax numbers and e-mail addresses which will assist in sales follow-up.

Lists can be obtained from a number of sources such as magazine and directory publishers – *Yellow Pages, Thomson Directories* etc., – as well as telephone service providers and the Royal Mail.

It is important to remember that most lists are provided for one-off use only. They will include a number of 'seeds' – names and addresses coded so that the list owners will know if a list has been used without permission and without payment. It is wise to check the usage restrictions when purchasing a list from an owner or an agent.

## The Message

Having purchased your list, you need to compose a sales letter. For some advertisers, copy-writing, especially within the disciplined structure of a sales letter, is extremely difficult.

The important thing to remember is that a sales letter is like a personal salesman. Some of the rules that apply to the salesman need also to apply to the sales letter.

*For example:*

◆ they both need to make a good impression at first sight

◆ their sales message should be expressed in terms the customer will understand

◆ the products or services they offer should respond to a specific customer need

◆ the benefits they have to sell should be clearly explained

There are nine key points you should remember when writing and distributing a sales letter:

1   **Think of a customer need you can satisfy**
    All marketing begins with the identification of a customer need.
    Think of what you do well and who will benefit from it.

2   **Begin your letter with some understanding of this need**
    Let your prospective customer know that you understand
    his/her problem.

3   **Explain simply and clearly how you can help**
    Having identified the problem, show that you know how to resolve it.

4   **Do not make any statements that are untrue**
    Once found out, you will never be able to re-establish credibility
    with your customer. It is certain that you will be found out.

5   **Do not make claims you cannot justify**
    It is pointless stating that you can perform certain tasks you
    are not qualified to undertake.

6   **Have your letter printed or copied onto good
    quality letterhead paper**
    You would want your salesman to look his/her best
    when first meeting a customer – so should your sales letter.

7   **Always use the Guild (or any other relevant, reputable
    organisation you belong to) logo on your stationery**
    The Guild logo will add prestige to your sales letter.
    Where appropriate, mention your Guild membership in your letter.

8   **Sign each letter personally, if possible**
    This is only practical for small mailings. For larger distribution,
    have your signature printed on your letter.

9   **Ensure that your letters are delivered by a reliable agent**
    If delivered by hand, ensure that your letters actually
    reach your prospective customers.

Examples of specimen sales letters follow on page 90. You may use these in whole or in part to promote your company's skills. They are quite different and written for very different purposes. But in each case the rules specified above have been followed.

The letter from John Smith is very simple and straightforward. Its purpose is to effect introductions in the area and, eventually, obtain new business. It begins with a simple introduction and explains very clearly the work John Smith is best qualified to undertake.

Membership of the Guild of Master Craftsmen is offered as endorsement and the Guild logo included as proof. The writer says that he is available to take on urgent work immediately, and then suggests that he will be there in the future if and when the need arises. "You never know when you might need the services of a good, economical, reliable plumber." A need has been identified and a solution offered.

Jack Black's letter is quite different. He begins by making a statement that few would argue with. We all take electricity for granted. But then asks what would happen if it went wrong? Having aroused the concern, Jack Black offers a solution. He offers to check the wiring in the prospect's house for an agreed fee.

Realising that the prospect may be concerned that he or she is then obligated to place any remedial work with Jack Black, the writer reinforces with a PS the message that no such obligation exists.

The letter from Sunshine Travel is opportunistic. Obviously written just after a very cold spell of weather, the company is offering to turn the dream of warmer climes into reality.

Examples of temperatures at typical holiday destinations are quoted, along with special holiday rates available through Sunshine Travel. Personally addressed to an existing customer list, the letter is written in a warm and friendly fashion to anyone seeking the holiday of their dreams. And not forgetting those who enjoy a winter holiday, the PS offers a special rate for an all-inclusive skiing holiday.

**John Smith (Plumbing) Ltd**
**57 Bromfield Road**
**SOUTH ENDEAN**
**Wessex BX1 3RU**

Dear Sir or Madam

My name is John Smith. I am a domestic plumber and a member of
The Guild of Master Craftsmen. I work hard, and provide quality
workmanship and prompt service at competitive prices. Few jobs are
too large, none are too small – from the installation of complete
central heating systems to fitting a new tap washer.

Perhaps you have a domestic plumbing problem which requires
attention right now. If so, why not give me a call? You will be under
no obligation, and an estimate will be provided for your approval
before work commences.

On the other hand, you may be thinking of plumbing work in the
weeks or months ahead. In that case it would probably make sense to
keep this letter handy for future reference. In fact, why not do that
anyway? **You never know when you might need the services of a**
**good, economical, reliable plumber.**

I hope that I may have the opportunity of working for you.

Yours sincerely

John Smith
Proprietor

**Jack Black (Electricians) Ltd
23 Coronation Road
LITTLECHESTER
North Cornwall RZ3 2LJ**

Dear Sir or Madam

It's a funny thing about electricity. We never even give it a second thought – until it goes wrong! But just imagine the disruption to your household if your electricity should fail tonight. No television, no washing machine, perhaps no cooking and, increasingly often, no heating. Electricity, it seems, is always there – until it goes wrong!

How long is it since your electric wiring was checked? In fact, has it ever been checked at all? I ask these questions because, if you do not know the answers, you may be interested in a special offer I am making to home owners in your area.

> **For just £X I will check the wiring in every room of a three or four-bedroom house. I will express a professional opinion as to its quality and safety. If it is satisfactory I will say so. If not, I will suggest remedial action and provide an estimate for the repair.**

Please give me a call on (01937) 22734. I will be very happy to arrange an appointment to visit you at your convenience.

Yours faithfully

Jack Black
Proprietor

**PS There is absolutely no obligation on your part to accept my estimate and you are, of course, free to obtain other opinions and estimates from anyone you choose.**

Sunshine Travel Ltd
97 High Street
WESTHAMPTON
West Suffolk KX10 3RG

Mr J E Thomas                                         16th February 2000
17 Lower West Drive
WESTHAMPTON
West Suffolk KX14 7FR


Dear Mr Thomas

**How did you manage during the recent cold spell?** Pretty awful
wasn't it? Hopefully you kept your central heating going indoors,
wrapped up warm outdoors – and dreamt of warmer climes
elsewhere. Very sensible. But why not turn that dream into reality?
You could you know – with Sunshine Travel.

Do you know that it was 21 degrees in Lanzarote last week?
And it would have cost you just £X per person self catering to have
been there all week with Sunshine Travel. Bermuda was even warmer
– 26 degrees. That would have been only £X half board for 14 nights
through Sunshine Travel. And in Singapore it was a sizzling 30
degrees. A very economical £X for 7 nights full board in a 4 star hotel
when booked through Sunshine Travel.

As you can see, we have holidays for every budget and every
occasion. So don't get left out in the cold. Call into the warm and
friendly offices of Sunshine Travel and see how we can assist you in
finding the holiday of your dreams. We're here to help.

Yours sincerely



Janet Williams
Manager


PS  If you actually like the snow and are thinking of a skiing holiday,
we have some wonderful bargains on 7-night all-inclusive holidays in
Jasper National Park, Alberta, Canada – from just £590. Price includes
flight, superior hotel accommodation, all food and all drink!

TLR Publishing Co. Ltd
62 West Street
Sutton Bridge
South Merseyside PQ1 7LF

20th May 2000

Dear Valued Customer

## NEW BOOK OFFER - SAVE 50%

As a regular purchaser of TLR books I would like to thank you in a
very special way for your custom and your support over the years. I
would also like to thank you in a very practical way – by making you
a unique offer.

Later this year we will be publishing a new book – Ray Johnson's
"Guide to Antique Valuation". You will know Ray Johnson from his
many television appearances as the leading technical expert in the
very popular programme: "Old and Valued". This new book, which
draws on all Ray's technical expertise, shows you how to place a
value on your old family heirlooms – and possibly some of the family
rubbish as well!

With more than 250 colour pages, 400 illustrations and 100 line
drawings, Ray Johnson's "Guide to Antique Valuation" is tremendous
value at the full published price of £19.95. For those we consider to
be our very best customers, this book is unbeatable value at £9.95.
All we ask is that you place your order before the end of June.

A leaflet is enclosed describing this new book in some detail. To take
advantage of this offer, simply complete the order form attached and
return with it along with your cheque or credit card details. It's your
way of saving 50% on a very special book, and it's our way of saying
"Thank You" for being a very special customer.

Yours faithfully


Gareth Jones
Special Products Manager


PS Don't forget that to take advantage of this offer you must confirm
your order before the end of June!

## Other Direct Response Advertising

Whenever you attempt to obtain a direct response from an advertisement, leaflet or reply card, you are involved in direct response advertising. This may also include loose-leaf inserts in magazines and/or newspapers.

More and more publications are now accepting loose inserts as publishers attempt to compete with the growth of direct mail, especially in the areas of the Internet and the fax machine.

Although advertisers know that some readers will shake the inserts out of a recently purchased magazine, the fact still remains that, on a cost-per-response basis, greater interest is usually recorded for this form of promotion, than for conventional display advertising.

Product cards are packs of cards printed with a simple sales message on one side and a postage-paid return address on the other. Printing costs are absorbed in the individual card rate, and packs are distributed by magazines to their own mailing lists. They are usually confined to business-to-business advertising and can be a very cost-effective means of reaching potential customers.

**Examples of effective direct marketing.**

*Above: A personal message of welcome ensures an understanding of customer needs in this direct mail catalogue.*

*Left: Effective use of the Guild logo plus an incentive will attract immediate attention.*

## SUMMARY

- Direct marketing is concerned with obtaining a response directly from the coupon, leaflet or reply card provided

- Direct response advertising on television is a major growth area

- Direct response advertising on the Internet will be a major growth market area in the near future

- Direct mail, accurately targeted, can never be described as 'Junk Mail'

- One of the secrets of direct mail advertising is establishing the right list and ensuring it is up to date

- A sales letter is like a personal salesman, and similar rules apply to both

- There are 10 key points to remember when writing and distributing a sales letter

- Inserts in publications usually produce a lower cost-per-response than display advertisements

- Product cards are an effective means of advertising business-to-business

# Public Relations

**12**

Whether or not we realise it, we all have an image. Sometimes it is a little off-putting when we come face-to-face with the image, seeing ourselves as others see us.

It is not too much of an exaggeration to say that our image is even more important than reality. If others see us as serious minded, they react to us as though we are serious minded, despite the fact that we believe ourselves to be, say, happy-go-lucky and humorous.

In the business world, companies have images, and, as most senior executives understand, it is crucially important that this public face coincides with the image of the company they want to project.

For example, it would be very bad today for a company to appear unconcerned about 'green' issues. With consumers now generally being more aware of environmental issues, they may decide not to purchase products or services from companies considered wasteful of scarce natural resources or those who appear to promote experimentation on animals.

The way our company image is perceived by customers and potential customers is a major part of business development, and if something should occur to affect that image, then immediate, and very public action is required, if lasting harm is not to be inflicted on our trading potential.

For example, one company is Surrey which unintentionally and inadvertently discharged industrial waste into a nearby river, killing off a quantity of frogs, actually went as far as importing other frogs to replace them – and, to make an announcement to that effect in the local newspapers.

This latter part of the exercise – making an announcement in the newspapers – is what most people think of as public relations.

In truth, public relations goes a great deal further than this. Its concern should be the formulation of policy. In the example of the Surrey company and the polluted river, that policy would have been the decision to replace the frogs in the first place.

To work properly, public relations should never be a by-product of a company's activities – it should be the reason for many of them.

## Media Relations

What most people consider public relations is, in fact, media relations – a strategy to obtain favourable references to the company and its products in media that is read and observed by the company's public e.g. customers, suppliers, investors etc.

The reasons for attempting such an exercise are twofold. First, if successful, it is a means of raising awareness of your company name and the services offered. Secondly, it is a means of obtaining free advertising. In truth, editorial space is a better salesman than an advertisement. It is the difference between you telling me how wonderful you are and someone else, independently, saying the same thing. Despite your well-deserved reputation for honesty, the latter is somewhat more believable.

## Why Press Releases Fail

It should be noted that not every press release that is written and sent to a newspaper, magazine or tv/radio station will make it past the waste paper bin in the editor's office. The reasons are numerous, but one question you should always ask, is, what's in it for the publications themselves?

The answer should be news, information and items of interest for their readers, viewers or listeners. So many times companies seeking publicity seem to forget this – because their press release is relevant to them, they believe it should appeal to others.

Often a moment's thought will show this is not so, and that there is absolutely no reason why any publication should print their release.

For example, one company in North America regularly sends a press release to newspapers around the world announcing the dates of their factory closedown for the various religious holidays. It may well justify a fee from the company's public relations agency, but it is doubtful if any publication outside the immediate area of the factory would be in the slightest bit interested.

To give another perspective to the potential problem areas, many leading magazine or newspaper editors will receive in excess of 1,000 press releases a week – only a very small percentage of this number will ever be printed.

*The main reasons for rejecting a press release include:*

- **irrelevant to the readership**
  A story about a new paint for boats being sent to a
  magazine on plumbing.

- **inappropriate for the publication**
  An item on ways to avoid VAT charges sent to an
  official Customs and Excise journal.

- **badly timed**
  Announcing the winning of a tender to build a new head office,
  when it has been completed and occupied.

- **without news value**
  Feature on the number of times the 'phone rings
  in customer services every week.

- **poorly written**
  Needs reading at least six times just to find out the
  name of the company sending the release

The average cost of writing and distributing a press release, including a photograph, is £6 each. It is estimated that about 97% of press releases are wasted. This means that a successful release will cost around £200 – still cost-effective in most media when compared to the cost for advertising, but no justification for companies wasting time and money writing and distributing irrelevant and inappropriate press releases.

## Writing a Good Press Release

The first thing any good press release should do is attract immediate attention. An editor faced with 1,000 releases a week, expecting most of them to be inappropriate and irrelevant, will not waste a lot of time reading each one.

If the release has not gained his/her attention in the first couple of sentences, then it is more than likely going to end up in the recycling paper bin.

Press releases should not be long and laboured. They should consist of short, punchy sentences, each one about 15 or 20 words long, in tight paragraphs. The whole story should be captured in no more than 250 words. In that space all the questions relating to who, what, why, when, where and how should be answered.

*To be successful, a press release should have the following:*

- a headline that attracts attention
- a first paragraph that contains the main points of the release in no more than 50 words
- a body text that is relevant, not repetitious, flowing and not flowery
- points that are easy to understand and unambiguous
- short, rather than long, difficult-to-understand words
- use of plain English
- words that relate to the picture, if one is included
- the name of the product or service
- the important features of the product or service
- believable content
- contact name for further information
- the date of issue of the release

## Distributing a Press Release

It is estimated that there are some 12,000 different media outlets for your press release in the UK alone. About half of these are trade, technical and professional magazines and newspapers. Covering all of them, even at £6 a time, would be costly, extremely wasteful and above all pointless.

Commonsense dictates that only those newspapers, magazines, tv and radio stations likely to have some interest in the subject matter of the release should receive it.

There are many sources of names and addresses for all media outlets. The most famous of these for media in the UK is BRAD, which is published monthly. It is a publication used by advertising agencies as it gives full details of the media in question – rates for advertising, contact names and addresses, areas of specific interest and circulation figures.

Individual copies are rather expensive to buy, but they may be seen in the reference section of most public libraries.

The press release itself should be typed double-spaced, preferably, but not necessarily, on a single sheet. A photograph should be included, whenever possible, and sent in a protective envelope. The envelope should be addressed to the editor by name (correctly spelt), if possible, hand-written, but certainly not impersonally addressed to the editor on a computer label.

Where considered particularly relevant to the publication in question, it may help to 'phone ahead advising them that the release has been dispatched, and to follow that with a later call to ensure that it arrived safely.

## PRESS RELEASE

*press notice*

### LOCAL BUSINESS ACHIEVES NATIONAL RECOGNITION

(Your name here), a local company employing skilled local labour, has recently been awarded membership of the Guild of Master Craftsmen. Membership was granted by the Guild's Council of Management in recognition of the company's commitment to work with skill and integrity, and its agreement to abide by the Guild's publicly declared aims and objectives. This follows approval of references submitted by a number of (your business name here) satisfied customers. The company is now entitled to display the Guild logo at its premises, on company vehicles and all stationery items.

Membership of the Guild of Master Craftsmen offers many benefits to those able to satisfy the selection criteria. These include assistance in marketing skills and techniques, recommendations and advice for managing a growing business, and participation in many specially negotiated cost-reduction schemes.

A national organisation, with members in many different trades, crafts and vocations, the Guild welcomes applications for membership from suitably qualified individuals and organisations.

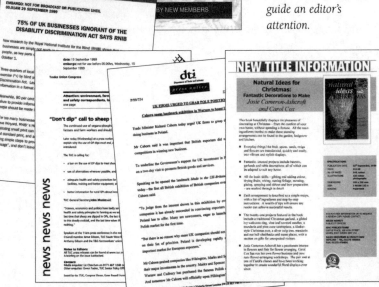

*A selection of press releases showing various layouts and styles to immediately guide an editor's attention.*

## SUMMARY

- Companies, like individuals, have an image. This is important to the way customers and suppliers react to them.

- Public relations should never be a by-product of a company's activities, but an active agent in formulating company policy.

- Media relations exist to promote the company to existing and potential customers.

- If successful, media relations is an additional form of advertising. It can also be more cost effective.

- Press releases should be relevant, appropriate, correctly timed, newsworthy and well-written.

- Most press releases are wasted because they do not attract attention in the first two or three sentences.

- Only media likely to be interested in the subject matter should be sent a press release.

# The People:
# Retain, Recruit or Outsource?

13

The ability to satisfy the needs of the customer, and fulfil your promises to them, depends on a number of important factors. One of the most important is staff. You might need to take on additional people or simply utilise your existing staff in a more effective way. It is worth remembering that if you have not recruited the right people for the job, or they are not happy in their work, your business will suffer. No amount of marketing activity will compensate for ineffective staff.

## Retaining

Sir John Harvey Jones is quoted as saying: "It's amazing that people put retention of staff so low on the agenda". This is true, even though most people are aware that the cost of retaining staff is far less than the cost of recruiting new staff. Essentially, retention comes down to that much over-used (and much misunderstood) word – motivation.

Contrary to common belief, motivation is not 'getting the best out of people'. It is helping people to get the best out of themselves. In fact, behavioural psychologists would tell us that it is physically impossible to motivate another person. But what we can do is create an environment in which they can motivate themselves. Those same psychologists tell us that most people work at less than 50 % of their potential and use less than 5% of their brain power.

This leaves lots of room for improvement, suggesting that investment in a highly motivational environment is a very cost-effective investment. For the last half century, management gurus such as MacGregor, Maslow, Hertzberg, Drucker and more recently, Tom Peters and Robert Heller, have studied motivation – and all have come to the same conclusion. That is that most people feel unfulfilled because they are not able to give their best and believe that they could contribute far more if only they were allowed to. The reason is because most organisations unknowingly build barriers to motivation in their systems, structures and practices. Peter Drucker suggests two questions which every manager should ask in an effort to improve motivation. The first is 'What should I do to help you become more effective'; the second is, 'What should I stop doing to help you become more effective'!

Dismantling the barriers to self-motivation is simple – but not easy. It is simple because it is logical – but it is difficult because it demands time and effort from the manager, and probably confrontation with peers who have long resisted change. Change must start at the top – the chief executive. Whether they know it or not, they set the standards for what happens in their organisation by their own personal behaviour. The following steps will contribute to a highly motivational environment.

### SHOW THAT YOU CARE

Research shows that people will give more effort and commitment if they feel that they are valued and cared for. In a motivational environment, the manager or team leader takes a greater personal interest in the team members than anyone else would. They listen to, and value, their opinions. In fact, they apply the golden rule 'treat others as you would like to be treated'.

### LET THEM OWN THEIR JOBS

People like to feel that they own the job they do. The power of ownership is a great motivator – it provides authority, responsibility and accountability.

### LET THEM USE THEIR TALENT

A motivational environment liberates people to use their talent and achieve their potential. It encourages self motivation, self assessment and self confidence.

### LET THEM TAKE RISKS

People won't be risk takers unless they are in a trusting environment. An environment which damns failure and encourages blame, stifles initiative.

### PROTECT THEIR DIGNITY

Everyone should respect each other's self-image, self-esteem and most of all dignity. Many working environments are corrupted by cynicism. Cynicism and contempt can be overcome by encouraging mutual respect – and the first step to earning respect is giving it.

These behavioural steps can be supplemented with a system which rewards effort and achievement – in other words, rewards what they do, not what their job specification says they should do.

Most assets in an organisation depreciate. People are one of the few assets that can appreciate. Your people will grow and contribute far more in a highly motivational environment, if they stay long enough?

## Recruiting or Outsourcing

Retaining staff is not an easy task, but it becomes a lot simpler if you can recruit the right staff from the beginning.

Maintaining staff, however many that might be, is not an easy task, but it becomes a lot simpler if you can recruit the right staff from the outset.

It is important to remember that finding an employee who is the best fit for your company will increase the likelihood of a long and fruitful working relationship.

So how do you go about finding the right person for your company? There are a few key steps that should be followed which have been proven to reduce the risk of appointing the wrong person.

**Advertising** – Aim to attract quality candidates by targeting your advertising to the right market. For example, if the position to be filled is professionally orientated, then use a specialist magazine or newspaper. If it is more general, then use a good circulation local paper.

**Prepare a person specification** – Be realistic about who you are looking for and describe your ideal candidate on paper. Are there any special skills/qualifications required in the job? If you need someone who can take on a broad range of jobs, or requires a sense of humour, then say so. Now divide the list into those qualities that are essential (and those that are desirable) for the 'perfect' recruit.

Having sifted through the applications, the next stage is to create a shortlist of potential candidates. Then, 'that' moment has arrived – the interview. For many employers, the prospect can be very daunting. Don't despair, take it calmly and plan each stage.

**The interview area layout** – You don't need an interview room, pulling up two chairs at a 45 degree angle is quite acceptable. If you have to sit at a desk, try to sit side-on to the candidate. Placing the desk between you produces a barrier which makes it difficult for the interviewee to relax.

**Relax their thinking** – Ensuring that the interviewee is comfortable and relaxed will mean that they are able to give of their best, so begin by asking some general questions. This enables them to settle.

**Use open questions** – These allow you to 'draw out' the interviewee. Closed questions can only be answered yes or no. Instead ask, "You obviously found us. Which way did you come?" This leaves plenty of scope for discussing their journey and you may learn some interesting information such as where they live, whether they drive, etc.

**Sexual discrimination** – Do not leave yourself open to an accusation of sexual discrimination. There are few jobs where only one sex may be openly recruited. Also be aware of not asking sexually discriminating questions, for example, "Who will look after your children while you are at work?"

**Asking awkward questions** – You may need to ask awkward or embarrassing questions, for example "DO YOU HAVE A CRIMINAL RECORD?". Always be clear why you're asking such a question and what you hope to gain from the reply.

**References** – Always take up references in writing, preferably followed by a telephone reference. It makes sense to contact the referees by telephone and ask one or two other searching questions, such as the candidate's attendance record.

**The job offer** – Under English Law a verbal contract is binding, so be careful not to indicate a job offer until you have chosen the candidate. It should then be followed up in writing. State a trial period. People are not always as they presented themselves at interview and you may need a legitimate get-out clause several weeks later.

**Employment Law** – It is very helpful if you have a knowledge about employment legislation.

As mentioned earlier, your employment procedures will need to take into account the principle of equality in the workplace. The relevant laws are:

*The Sex Discrimination Act 1975 & 1986*

*The Race Relations Act 1976*

*The Disability Discrimination Act 1995*

*The Trade Union & Labour Relations (Consolidation) Act 1992*

Having taken on a new member of staff, there is a legal obligation to provide them, within two months of the start date, with a statement of the main terms and conditions of their contract of employment.

*The particulars must include:*

Names of the parties

Employment start date and any period of continuous employment

Rate of remuneration, method of calculation
(where appropriate) together with frequency of payment

Hours of work, holiday entitlement, sick leave,
sick pay and any pension terms

Notice period – both employee and employer

Place of work

Period for the job, if not permanent,
or when any fixed term is to end

Details of disciplinary rule and grievance procedures

Full details where the employee is required to work
outside the UK for more than one month.

It is worth bearing in mind that an employee who has been employed continuously by their employer for at least one year, regardless of the number of hours worked each week, have certain rights. These include the right not to be unfairly dismissed and the right to receive statutory redundancy pay. Since 1999, employees have been entitled to a minimum hourly rate of pay, so be sure that you are aware of, and comply with that legislation.

An alternative to recruiting personnel to satisfy the demands of an increasing order book, or to meet specific demands from one particular customer, is to use contract or temporary staff. Basically, there are no legal restrictions in the UK to the use of this type of labour.

## Outsource

Temps are mainly employed by recruitment agencies and are usually charged out to their clients at an hourly, weekly or monthly rate. Employed on this basis, the temp would not be part of your staff and as a result you would not be responsible for keeping payroll records, deducting PAYE and National Insurance costs, etc. You would simply pay the agency for the time worked by the temp.

In many cases the temp can provide an effective, productive and reliable solution to many employment requirements. The most obvious is to cover for increased workload at particularly busy periods. Temps have been used most frequently in recent years for the implementation and maintenance of computer systems, as well as credit control and debt collection, where the temp's knowledge from working with various companies experiencing widely varying problems has proven to be invaluable and cost effective.

Of course temporary staff are ideal to cover for illness, maternity leave, unfilled permanent positions and long-term holidays.

The use of contract personnel is another means of utilising the best skills, without the management burdens incurred with permanently employed staff. It is an area that is growing and is likely to continue growing for many years as businesses examine their operations to identify where they should be focusing their management efforts, and what are their peripheral activities. Such peripheral activities generally demand a disproportionate amount of management time and effort and often are undertaken in an inefficient manner.

In response to this problem, organisations are taking the option of using contract labour or even outsourcing some, or all, of these activities to specialist service providers who possess the latest skills; employ the best practices and attain economies of scale by undertaking the same type of work for a number of clients.

The list of activities for outsourcing can be long and it is for each organisation to identify which activities could be safely developed to an external contractor.

Traditional candidates include security services, catering and cleaning, but nowadays other support activities, such as audit, computing support, customer help desks, finance, marketing, information technology, payroll, personnel and purchasing are increasingly being entrusted to external specialists.

Outsourcing forces a careful examination of the service in question which can often lead to a re-engineering of that function and the way other business functions interact with it.

Whether or not the subject of outsourcing is a function, such as cleaning, or a service such as computing, there are a number of points that need attention. *These are:*

**Service description** – This is the description of the service that is required to be provided. It should be clear, concise and avoid ambiguities.

**Choosing a contractor** – Before inviting potential contractors, you need to be sure that you are only dealing with those organisations best equipped to handle your needs. Decide clear objectives then issue a questionnaire to as many likely companies as you can sensibly identify.

**T.U.P.E.** – You need to consider if the Transfer of Undertakings Protection of Employment applies to the function you wish to outsource. If it does, then appropriate consultations with the staff currently engaged upon the work will need to be undertaken.

**Terms & conditions** – You need to be sure the contract will be subject to terms and conditions that provide for safeguards that are appropriate to your organisation. Issue your own.

**Timetables** – The process is not necessarily a quick one. If an unrealistic timetable is set, it will lead to corners being cut with errors being made and misunderstandings arising.

## SUMMARY

- Contrary to common belief, motivation is not 'getting the best out of people'. It is helping people to get the best out of themselves

- Change must start at the top – the chief executive

- A motivational environment liberates people to use their talent and achieve their potential

- People are one of the few assets that can appreciate

- Aim to get quality candidates by targeting your advertising to the right market

- Be realistic about who you are looking for and describe your ideal candidate on paper

- Do not leave yourself open to an accusation of sexual discrimination

- Always take up references in writing, preferably followed by a telephone reference

- It is very helpful if you have a knowledge about employment legislation

- An alternative to recruiting personnel to satisfy the demands of an increasing order book, is to use contract or temporary staff

- The temp can provide an effective, productive and reliable solution to many employment requirements

- Using contract personnel is another means of utilising the best skills, without the management burdens incurred with permanently employed staff

# Professional Help

14

It is often the case that young businesses, are managed by men and women with a special talent in one specific management discipline. For example, if the business is technical, it is likely to have a technical specialist at the helm. Likewise, if it is sales-based, it is probably led by someone who has climbed the ladder through sales management.

It would be unwise and unrealistic to expect these people suddenly to become wizards in the world of finance, corporate strategies or even business consultants, simply because they have decided to start a business in which they are technically competent.

Obviously, extra management skills are acquired over a period of time, as learning by doing and learning by mistakes are inevitable, but there are certain to be moments when expert professional help is desperately needed.

But where exactly should a harassed executive look for marketing or other forms of professional help and advice?

## First Steps

It is a matter of fact that every business has objectives. They may not always be openly stated, but they are there nevertheless. Spending a little time formulating and quantifying these objectives is necessary as a first step, before any professional help can be considered.

Perhaps the intention is to increase your sales by 10% in real terms over the next 12 months and you have a specific sum of money available to achieve this. If so, you should express it, clearly and precisely, without fear of any misunderstandings.

Your goal may be unrealistic in terms of your advertising budget, but better to find that out at the beginning than vaguely stating that all you want is to 'get some more money from an increase in business'.

Designers and others have often been accused of overcharging, when they have assumed (in the absence of any clear advice from their clients to the contrary) that there were no specific restrictions on the money to be spent. The result is that they have designed a Rolls-Royce, when a Lada was all that was required. Companies have a right to worry about professional specialists who spend clients' money as though drawing from a bottomless well of gold coins. But, the only sensible way to combat this is to express, right from the outset, your clear objectives, when they have to be achieved and the maximum budget.

## Finding Help

There are a number of formal bodies for most groups of professional advisers offering specialist skills. The Guild of Master Craftsmen has directories detailing these and can supply lists if needed. It may be that your business is eligible for government or EU assistance under a training initiative or export support scheme – it is worth checking with the Department of Trade to make certain.

Apart from these routes, you may find help from referral by others. Professional advisers rely on recommendations from satisfied customers in exactly the same way as you do. It might be worthwhile asking around your local business community to see if there is anyone who can offer you sound professional help.

*Before meeting a potential adviser you should:*

◆ produce a summary of what your business does

◆ produce a summary of your objectives

◆ produce your plans, insofar as they are defined

◆ produce a draft of your requirements

*At the first meeting you should ensure that:*

◆ the adviser understands your business

◆ the adviser provides references of work in related businesses – ideally not competitive

◆ the adviser provides a copy of his contractual terms and conditions

*After the meeting the adviser should:*

◆ provide a full explanation of the services he expects to supply, clearly setting out his understanding

◆ provide an estimate, a timetable and a payment schedule

◆ send a contract for your acceptance and signature

You may find it necessary to go through that process more than once. It is worthwhile ensuring that you establish a link with a business you can work with.

Once you have entered into a contract, it is important that the adviser presents an outline of proposals at an early stage, including, where appropriate, drawings and rough work for your consideration.

This should give you peace of mind, as you can see his/her thinking in action before too many costs are incurred.

## Advertising Agencies

It is wrong to believe that all advertising agencies are only interested in major accounts who spend large sums of money. Many agencies are small themselves and are anxious to take on small, ambitious clients they can grow with.

The services they offer may not all be in-house; freelancers are frequently employed to provide artwork, design and copywriting. At the very least, though, even the smallest agency should provide a proposed advertising budget, outlining all the costs you are likely to incur in achieving your advertising objectives, for you to approve.

Advertising agencies should be able to explain how these objectives will be achieved, the creative approach they propose for the planned campaign, the reasons why certain magazines or newspapers have been selected, what leaflets will be printed and how, and to whom they will be distributed, and so on.

It is up to you as the client to question the decisions made and possibly provide your own suggestions, especially where trade and technical publications are proposed, as you may well have far more knowledge of the marketplace than the advertising agency.

## Design Studios

Sometimes companies prefer to go directly to the specialist and leave out the intermediary. Design studios are more than capable of interpreting designs for advertisements and printed literature. Once again, maximum expenditure levels and clear objectives should be established, and clearly explained at the outset, if shocks are to be avoided at the invoicing stage.

## Guild Sales and Marketing Services

Frequently The Guild of Master Craftsmen is contacted by members who are anxious to obtain wider-ranging marketing advice than simply advertising and design. This help can be provided where the request is clearly presented in writing with as much background information as possible. The nature of the problem should be identified, and solutions already attempted be outlined. Armed with details of all the known facts, a really practical and effective response can be made.

## Business Counselling

There are times when The Guild is approached by members whose whole business requires the close scrutiny of a number of experts. The Guild therefore operates a Business Counselling Scheme for just this purpose.

The member is encouraged to complete a comprehensive questionnaire which, for a small fee, is scrutinised by business leaders who are experts in marketing, finance, sales, property, taxation or insurance. Sound advice is given and solutions proposed.

*Design studios can interpret ideas into designs for advertisements and printed literature.*

# SUMMARY

● Business leaders do not always have all the management skills necessary to operate a successful business.

● Marketing specialists are sometimes required to provide professional help and advice.

● The best results are obtained when marketing objectives are identified and quantified prior to seeking professional help.

● Advertising agencies should provide a complete service, from preparing a budget and promoting a campaign, to the creation of advertisements and their placement.

● Design studios are capable and willing to interpret a brief and provide designs for advertisements and printed literature.

● The Guild of Master Craftsmen provides sales and marketing advice to its members on request.

● The Guild's comprehensive Business Counselling Scheme looks at marketing, finance, sales, property, taxation and insurance.

# Trade Associations

15

Earlier, in Chapter 8, we discussed the subject of selling the product. The importance of making the right first impression was emphasised. Then, later in the book, when considering public relations, the importance of a company's image was discussed, along with how image affects the way customers view the company, and the products and services it offers.

These various factors, combined with membership of the right trade association can support and enhance a company's marketing efforts and help promote the correct image to customers and potential customers.

## Endorsements

Celebrities, especially those we see regularly on our tv screens, are often paid large sums of money to promote or endorse particular products. The reason for this is very simple and straightforward – endorsements, especially by someone we know and trust, work.

We may feel sceptical about the claims made in these advertisements, but the fact remains that they really do work. Sometimes the endorsement is not a direct one. Products used in films and soap operas, clothing and equipment used and worn by sports stars, even the Royal Warrant on a bottle or jar are all subtle endorsements, that encourage consumers to buy certain products in preference to others.

For example, tv cook Delia Smith hit the headlines – and not for the first time – when in a short series of programmes she used accessories and ingredients, which were then in turn quickly purchased by her millions of viewers. The result was that the suppliers of these products and ingredients had a manic task just trying to keep pace with the sudden influx of demand. One company sold more of its particular accessory in a single week than its had previously sold over a three-year trading period.

When you stop and think about it, why shouldn't they? The first products we buy, as young men and women, are invariably recommended by parents and friends. These recommendations encourage an element of trust which is so essential in making a successful sale. This trust is essential not only before the sale, but afterwards too.

Market research has shown that the majority of new car advertisements were viewed or read about by those who had recently purchased the same car. These were consumers looking for confirmation that the purchase they had made was the right one.

Any company wishing to increase its sales would be wise to consider any promotional aid that endorses its products both before and after the sale.

## Joining a Trade Association

When a company joins a trade association, it differentiates itself from those who do not belong. Automatically a new dimension is added to the company's sales message – it is like being told that a certain individual you recently met belongs to a trade union, supports a particular football club or attends a certain university.

This new knowledge may well change your perception of that individual, hopefully for the better, sometimes the reverse. That is why the decision to join one trade association, in preference to another, is so important for the future of your company and its development.

For example, if you are a widget manufacturer, membership of the Association of Widget Manufacturers will inform potential customers of what you do. Unfortunately, it will not tell them how well you do it. This is where the Guild of Master Craftsmen offers so much more in the way of customer security and trust.

## Customer Satisfaction

The Guild of Master Craftsmen is different from most other trade associations for two distinct reasons. First, before membership is approved, the Guild always insists on receiving recommendations from recently satisfied customers. Just think about this aspect for a moment, from a potential customer's point of view. To a new customer, this is very much like receiving an endorsement from a neighbour or friend, and is a very important point which all Guild members are encouraged to include in every single sales presentation.

Secondly, the Guild operates a recognised complaints procedure where any dispute between a Guild member and his/her customer is objectively and resolutely pursued until both sides are totally satisfied with the proposed solution.

This objective approach is the customer's guarantee that his/her interests are taken into consideration, and this in turn enhances the confidence that the customer needs before deciding where to place his/her order.

The Guild was established to promote those companies and individuals who take pride in what they do and act with honesty and integrity when dealing with customers. One of the published aims of the Guild is 'TO PROTECT THE PUBLIC BY INSTILLING AMONG MEMBERS A GREATER SENSE OF RESPONSIBILITY, MAKING MEMBERS AWARE OF THE NATIONAL IMPORTANCE OF THE SERVICES THEY RENDER — AND BY ENCOURAGING MEMBERS ALWAYS TO STRIVE FOR EXCELLENCE'.

In placing customer satisfaction so firmly in the forefront of its objectives, the Guild believes it is assisting its members in the marketing of the products and services they sell.

## Promotional Material

There is an old adage in the advertising business that says 'you can't sell if you don't tell'. This is especially true in the use members of trade associations make of their association or Guild logo.

To help its members obtain the best possible marketing potential, a whole range of promotional material featuring the Guild logo is available to members. These will help support initial sales contact, where an introductory letter may be accompanied by an identity/compliments slip listing the aims of the Guild, right through to aftersales reassurance, where the invoice arrives in an envelope overprinted with the Guild logo.

In the interim the member can reinforce the message of quality with many other items, from ties and brooches to overall and blazer badges and from window and product stickers to van signs and contract boards. The range of promotional items is continually being increased to ensure the reputation of the member in the marketplace is constantly enhanced in an ever evolving business environment.

## Guild News

Throughout this book the importance of advertising and promotion has been stressed time and again. It is a vital part of every company's marketing mix. To assist its members further, the Guild of Master Craftsmen encourages its members to advertise in Guild publications, offering them very favourable rates – generous discounts on display advertising, and helping with the design and origination of both display and classified advertising.

The range of publications produced by the Guild is constantly being expanded and developed. It covers a wide range of professional, trade and hobby interests including all aspects of woodworking, gardening, photography, needlecrafts, dolls' house and miniatures and crafts for the home, plus the exclusive Guild membership magazine, *Guild News*.

This magazine provides an excellent opportunity for members to offer discounts to other members on the goods and services they supply. Members regularly advertise to other members through its pages.

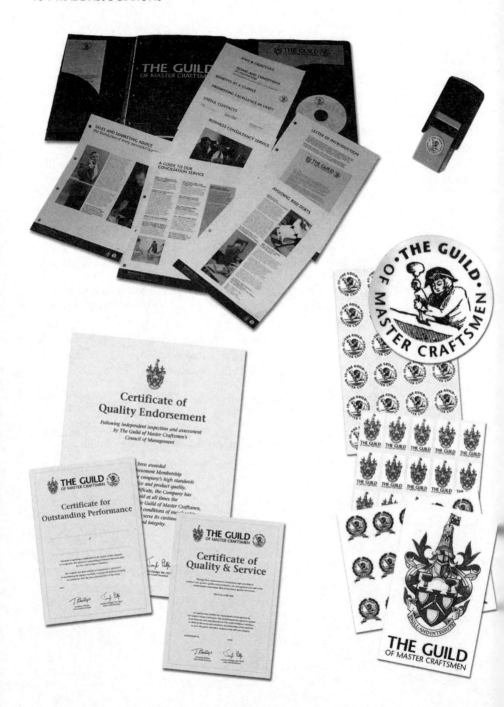

## Guild News

## Other Guild Magazines

## SUMMARY

- Guild membership supports and enhances a company's own marketing efforts.

- Recommendations from other satisfied customers encourage trust and increase the opportunities to sell.

- Aftersales reassurance confirms the decision made by the customer to purchase a particular product or service.

- Membership of a trade association, that emphasis the quality of its members' work, is reassuring to potential customers.

- Marketing seeks customer satisfaction, which is in the forefront of the Guild's aims and objectives.

- Guild promotional material allows members to exploit membership at every possible opportunity.

- The Guild encourages all members to advertise in its publications at generously discounte d rates.

# The Marketing Plan

Marketing is more than a solitary management discipline. It interacts with every other aspect of the business and, in a truly marketing-oriented company, it is the cement which binds together all the resources in a totally integrated system. Because senior management is responsible for developing and running the company as a total entity – one which satisfies customers needs at a profit – a truly marketing-oriented company can only exist with full encouragement and support from the top.

This means that the corporate objectives and strategy have to be clearly defined at the start. The marketing plan is the road map to guide you in achieving those objectives. Like any other road map it will be even more useful if you regularly refer back to it during your journey to success.

## Preparing a Plan

This may seem daunting to the owner of a small company, but it needn't be. It can be as simple or complex as you choose. A large company with a professionally trained marketing department may produce a marketing plan which is 75 mm thick and forms a major part of the annually updated five-year corporate plan. Whereas a small company with only a few employees may produce a document of just a few pages. But for both of them, large and small, success necessitates deciding where they want to be at the end of the year, or some other predetermined period, and agreeing the necessary goals and strategy to take them there. This planning process should involve key staff (the people who are going to make it happen) to be sure that there is commitment to, and understanding of, the plan.

## The Plan

There are many different ways of preparing a marketing plan. The diagram below shows a simplified plan which is based on the format used by some multi-national organisations. and yet is equally effective with a two or three person company. The headings have been crossed referenced with relevant chapters in this book to clarify and simplify the decision making process.

**The Marketing Plan**

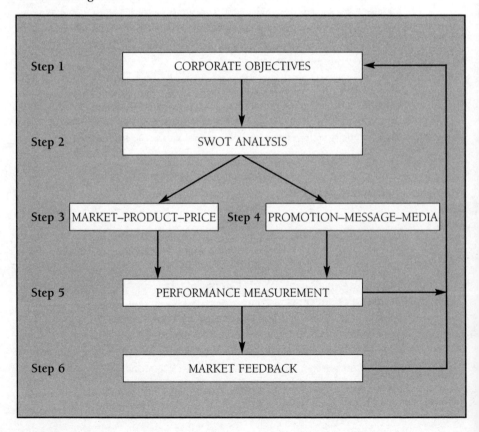

## STEP 1
## SET THE CORPORATE OBJECTIVES

It is necessary for the company owner or senior executives to decide how they want the company to develop in the foreseeable future. Basically this involves asking three questions;

◆ Where are we now?

◆ Where do we intend to be?

◆ When do we intend to be there?

It is not possible to produce a marketing plan without the answers to these questions.

## STEP 2
## ANALYSE YOUR STRENGTHS AND WEAKNESSES (SWOT ANALYSIS)

What will help us, or hinder us, in being successful? Completing the exercise shown in Chapter 1 will give you an overview of your organisational strengths and weaknesses and, even more important, lead you to determine the actions necessary to capitalise on your strengths and overcome or compensate for your weaknesses.

## STEP 3
## ANALYSE YOUR MARKET

This involves analysing your present situation and deciding what you need to do in these three areas to achieve the corporate objective. This analysis can be as brief or as detailed as you choose. Even an apparently superficial analysis can be very valuable in preparing the plan.

### Market (Chapter 4)

Many small companies feel inhibited by their lack of knowledge about the market and its various segments. And yet, you can be almost certain that you have a lot more knowledge within your organisation – if you look for it. This can be uncovered through simple brain-storming sessions with key personnel from various functions within the organisation (sales, production, finance, technical etc; the greater the mix the better). You can address questions relating to the areas where you feel you do have inadequate information.

Everyone will have a view, and even those who feel they have little knowledge may suggest a source through which that knowledge can be obtained. You can also address questions where you feel you have adequate information – some of your assumptions may be wrong! The following are examples of questions to be addressed in brain-storming:

◆ *What is the size of the market?*

◆ *What is our market share?*

◆ *Who are our major competitors – what is their market share?*

◆ *How could our market be segmented?*

◆ *Why do people buy from us?*

You will soon uncover other relevant questions to be addressed in building up knowledge of the market. Brain-storming really works, and in addition to exposing the knowledge that was locked in the heads of your colleagues, it motivates them by helping them to feel involved in the future development of the company.

### Product (Chapter 5)

We need to examine our existing product or service range, establish where it is in its life cycle and decide if the life cycle could be extended with cost effective modifications. Next we need to establish the potential for:

◆ Selling more existing products to existing customers

◆ Selling existing products to new customers

◆ Selling new products to existing customers

◆ Selling new products to new customers.

### Price

As addressed in Chapter 6, the pricing of your products or service is critical in terms of its acceptance by the customer and the impact on your profitability. In setting prices, we must always bear in mind the pricing paradox. A reduction in price can sometimes lead to a reduction in sales because of perceived cheapness, whereas an increase in price can sometimes lead to an increase in sales because of perceived value. (See case history 'Difficult pricing decisions on page 49') In essence, Step 3 involves producing a credible, but flexible, market – product – price strategy.

## STEP 4
## ANALYSE YOUR PROMOTION

This involves identifying a promotion strategy as outlined in Chapter 7. Sales promotion can be expensive – but it is necessary. When people feel that they have a product or service that will sell itself they are invariably failing to capitalise on the true potential. This is fine if it is in line with the corporate objectives. However, businesses which plan to grow need to promote themselves. Do you have a message? Should you develop a message? Do you have a Vision or Mission Statement which encapsulates the reason for the existence of your company and what it can contribute to its customers, suppliers and employees? This can be a useful source for a company or product message which will make your customers aware of you and inspire them to invest in your products or services.

## STEP 5
## MEASURE YOUR PERFORMANCE

In essence, a marketing plan is a dream – a dream of what could be achieved. Unfortunately, a dream without targets and performance measurement will remain a dream. Step 5 involves developing a timetable, setting a budget and allocating roles and responsibilities. In addition, you need to develop Plan B – your contingency for when things don't go in accordance with the plan!

You need to identify your Critical Success Factors (CSFs) – the elements which will have a major influence on the outcome of your plan. These will relate to targeted sales, expenditure and performance levels for all elements of the plan. You may extend this to cost per sale – sales per customer etc. Only you can decide the CSFs for your business. Wherever possible, the targets should cover a range rather than be a specific figure. Regular monitoring is essential and some targets will need to be monitored monthly, some weekly, and some even daily. This enables the marketing executive to assess the progress being made and make remedial decisions where necessary. The golden rule for John Cahill, a past Chief Executive of BTR was "no surprises!" He felt that if he had early warning of things going wrong he could minimise damage and, perhaps, turn things round.

If performance measurement is important to major corporations, it is equally important to even the smallest company. There are many performance indices to measure, but you should not fall into the trap of measuring for measurement's sake. The procedure should include only those elements which can have a critical impact on the success of the plan.

## STEP 6
## MARKET FEEDBACK (LISTEN TO THE MARKETPLACE)

Step 5 involved feedback from within the organisation. Equally important is feedback from outside the organisation – the marketplace. You need to know how well your company, product or service is being received by your customers and certain aspects need to be monitored on a regular basis. You also need to know how well your competitors are performing, whether new competitors are entering the market and whether your market segments are expanding or contracting (Chapter 4).

You should not rely solely on your salespeople for this information and again, involving people from other functions can be very beneficial. There is information that a finance person can obtain from another finance person that would never be given to a salesperson. There is information that a technical person can obtain from another technical person that would never be given to a salesperson. This applies to customers, competitors and outside agencies.

In addition, there is no substitute for the valuable information that can be obtained by your chief executive contacting the chief executive of a customer or a competitor. Again, knowledge is power and information is knowledge. Invariably, the information is available and all you need is a system for gathering it and feeding it back. This is the final step and, in effect, closes the loop in a simple marketing plan.

# A Practical Example

*Consider for a moment the practical construction of a very simple marketing plan. The example given is purely hypothetical and is intended to show how details may be gathered to be added to the marketing grid. The amount of detail finally included will depend on many factors.*

*It is worth pointing out here that it is always tempting to continue collecting new facts as long as we are working with incomplete information. What we have to remember is that marketing is not an exact science. In addition, the collation of information can be an excuse for delaying implementation, or an unwillingness to face up to the resulting success or failure of the plans. The rule to remember is that information is no longer valuable when its cost exceeds the savings it might bring.*

*Imagine then, a manufacturer of Frisbees. In our hypothetical example we will assume the company has recently produced a new and different version of this familiar product. For the purpose of our marketing plan, we may also assume that he is looking for large volume sales from a mass market. To sell in quantity he knows that his new product must sell for less than £10.*

*He will begin by putting his corporate objectives in writing (Step 1) then conducting the SWOT analysis with his key staff (Step 2). In Step 3 he will record that he is addressing a mass market which could easily be 'young men aged 18 to 25', 'housewives in Cumbria', or any other example of market segmentation, be it geographic, socioeconomic or lifestyle.*

*Under product, he will record that they have an innovative Frisbee which takes the enjoyment potential of this game to new levels. Under price, our Frisbee manufacturer will insert '£9.95'.*

*In Step 4 promotional opportunities could be display advertising, point of sale, radio and tv, direct mail and the Internet. Distribution channels will include toy shops, garages and similar retail outlet plus, perhaps, direct-to-user fulfilment.*

*When he considers media opportunities, our manufacturer may believe his product should be sold through certain newspapers and magazines with a strong youthful readership, certain independent radio and television stations and counter displays. In these media, he might anticipate offering an introductory discount off the recommended retail price. When considering the promotion of the new product in more detail, he might believe that only advertising in colour will illustrate the new product to its best advantage.*

*This would restrict the media opportunities to magazine and point of sale if television advertising and colour advertisements in newspapers were beyond the limits of his advertising budget. Direct mail might also be excluded at this stage, simply because order fulfilment of a comparatively low-priced item would be too costly. This would restrict the distribution channels to toy shops, garages and similar retail outlets.*

*As far as the message section is concerned, although not looking for a definite and final creative approach at this time, one promising idea from a brainstorming session might be a campaign built around the theme of 'Cheap Flights' combining the physical appeal of the product with its low price. This then suggests a change from the 10% off the introductory price offer, to a competition offering cheap flights on scheduled airlines to glamorous locations around the world. It is possible the campaign could be tied in with a particular scheduled airline who would offer fare concessions in exchange for the free promotion of their name. To make the most of this promotion, a specialist advertising agency might be engaged to develop a campaign which would help to pull the product through the distribution channels.*

*Step 5 is Performance Measurement. In making these preliminary suggestions for marketing this hypothetical product, we have tried to show how a detailed marketing plan can develop through the systematic approach outlined in this book. Eventually, a detailed plan will emerge with budgeted expenditure, targeted results and minimum performance levels. Sales territories, sales managers and representatives should all have expenditure levels and performance indices such as 'cost per sale', 'sales per month', and so on.*

*In Step 6 – Market Feedback, customer acceptance and actual performance levels will be fed back to see if adjustments may be necessary to the corporate objectives. Unless there is an extreme variation from budget, adjustments to the corporate objectives are very unlikely. However, if sales are way below budget, or much above, or if the actual rather than the budgeted cost of sales casts doubt on the financial viability of the product, the sooner this information is relayed back the quicker the organisation can adapt to these changed circumstances. As previously stated, feedback from the marketplace is crucial in any marketing-oriented company.*

# SUMMARY

- If you fail to plan – you are planning to fail.

- Marketing plans must begin with clearly defined corporate objectives.

- Marketing interacts with every other aspect of the business.

- The construction of a marketing plan should follow a systematic approach.

- Marketing is more than a solitary management discipline.

- New marketing initiatives will receive encouragement and support from senior management in marketing oriented companies.

- Corporate plan may have to be adjusted in line with the company's strengths, weaknesses, opportunities, threats – and events.

- Always have a 'Plan B' in readiness.

- Levels of actual performance must be compared with performance indices (CSFs) in the marketing plan.

- Constant and rapid feedback from the market place is necessary for a marketing-oriented company to adjust accurately its marketing plan in line with performance.

# Your Silent Partner

The Guild of Master Craftsmen is a marketing-oriented organisation which knows and understands many of the marketing problems of its members. The Guild assists members with the marketing of their products and services in three different ways:

1 The Guild provides specific marketing advice to individual companies where full details of any problem are analyised.

2 The Guild logo provides reassurance to customers, thus helping members to make the sale.

3 The Guild provides a range of benefits that save money and time, thus permitting members to use these two valuable commodities in the preparation of their own marketing programme.

The Guild is every member's 'silent partner'. A summary of the benefits currently available to members follows:


### PROFESSIONAL STATUS AND PUBLIC RECOGNITION
Guild members are recognised for their expertise and integrity. Membership clearly separates them from the inept, the uncaring and the unscrupulous.

### EXTRA BUSINESS POTENTIAL
Members of the public, businesses and institutions frequently contact the Guild, hoping to find a tradesman with a particular skill in their area.

### DEBT COLLECTION
A tried and tested scheme collects debts using a step-by-step procedure, from a formal solicitor's letter to an application for seizure of goods, with every stage priced separately.

## CONSUMER CREDIT CHECKS
Credit information on private individuals is available to members to reduce risk.

## FREE STATUS ENQUIRIES
Members contemplating long-term or exceptionally valuable contracts with other companies can obtain a number of free reports annually and others at competitive costs to help them make their decisions.

## FREE LEGAL ADVICE
Members can receive expert professional assistance and advice on all business and personal legal difficulties.

## SPECIAL INSURANCE SCHEMES
A broad range of insurance policies covering all aspects of business and personal life for Guild members, including:

◆ Group sickness and accident

◆ Public and employers' liability

◆ Business, commercial traders' and shopkeepers' insurance

◆ Goods in transit

◆ House, buildings and contents

◆ Private, commercial and fleet motor insurance

## THE GUILD LOGO AND COAT OF ARMS
The Guild logo and coat of arms are valuable trading assets. They enable potential customers to distinguish Guild members from others who could be unskilled and unqualified. The logos are featured on a wide range of promotional items.

## *YELLOW PAGES* AND *THOMSON* DIRECTORIES
Members may obtain listings in Guild corporate advertisements, enjoying the advantage of participation in a display advertisement at lineage rates and receiving public recognition for their skills.

## VEHICLE FINANCE AND MANAGEMENT OPTIONS
Hire purchase, contract hire and leasing schemes on all makes and models of vehicle, usually with considerable savings off the manufacturers list price.

## VEHICLE PURCHASE
Discounts on new vehicles are available from some leading manufacturers such as Ford, Renault and Volvo. Sometimes the benefit is enough to make the difference between a new or second hand purchase.

## CONCILIATION AND MEDIATION SERVICE
In all disputes between members and their customers, the Guild acts as an impartial third party, endeavouring to assist both sides in reaching an amicable settlement.

## FINANCIAL SERVICES
Advice is available for all financial services needs. Life assurance, income protection, pensions, investment planning, medical expenses cover and business finance.

## BUSINESS COUNSELLING
The Guild can offer sound ideas and suggestions to members for the improvement of their business from experts in marketing, finance, sales, property, taxation and insurance.

## SALES AND MARKETING SERVICES
Many members have received assistance from the Guild when confronted with specific sales and marketing problems.

## REGISTER OF MEMBERS
A database of members, classified by trade and geographical location, is maintained by the Guild in order to respond accurately to enquiries from members of the public, businesses and institutions.

## GUILD PUBLICATIONS
A generous 40% discount on all the Guild's best selling magazines and books is available to members.

## REDUCED ADVERTISEMENT RATES
Members may place classified advertising in all Guild magazines for a nominal fee covering just the typesetting charges. Display advertising is discounted in the Guild's members' magazine – *Guild News*.

## GUILD NEWS
The Guild publishes a regular magazine for members entitled *Guild News* which contains interesting and informative articles on matters closely affecting members and their businesses.

**MEMBER TO MEMBER DISCOUNTS**
Many members offer generous discounts on goods and services to other members.

**INTERNATIONAL DIVISION**
The Guild's International Division can put you in touch with sympathetic and allied craftsmen world-wide.

**CONTACT WITH OTHER CRAFTS**
Constant communication between members often leads to help and collaboration on specific projects.

**PROMOTIONAL MATERIAL**
A wide range of promotional material is available to help members sell their products and services.

**ADVERTISING FEATURES**
Regularly features are negotiated at special rates with local newspapers to promote the Guild and its members.

**CREDIT CARD FEES**
There are specially negotiated credit card merchant fees.

**GUILD FOR TODAY**
A 24-page colour guide describes all the Guild benefits and how to obtain them.

# Index

# TITLES AVAILABLE FROM GMC PUBLICATIONS

## Books

### Woodcarving

| | |
|---|---|
| Beginning Woodcarving | *GMC Publications* |
| Carving Architectural Detail in Wood: The Classical Tradition | *Frederick Wilbur* |
| Carving Birds & Beasts | *GMC Publications* |
| Carving Classical Styles in Wood | *Frederick Wilbur* |
| Carving the Human Figure: Studies in Wood and Stone | *Dick Onians* |
| Carving Nature: Wildlife Studies in Wood | *Frank Fox-Wilson* |
| Celtic Carved Lovespoons: 30 Patterns | *Sharon Littley & Clive Griffin* |
| Decorative Woodcarving (New Edition) | *Jeremy Williams* |
| Elements of Woodcarving | *Chris Pye* |
| Figure Carving in Wood: Human and Animal Forms | *Sara Wilkinson* |
| Lettercarving in Wood: A Practical Course | *Chris Pye* |
| Relief Carving in Wood: A Practical Introduction | *Chris Pye* |
| Woodcarving for Beginners | *GMC Publications* |
| Woodcarving Made Easy | *Cynthia Rogers* |
| Woodcarving Tools, Materials & Equipment (New Edition in 2 vols.) | *Chris Pye* |

### Woodturning

| | |
|---|---|
| Bowl Turning Techniques Masterclass | *Tony Boase* |
| Chris Child's Projects for Woodturners | *Chris Child* |
| Decorating Turned Wood: The Maker's Eye | *Liz & Michael O'Donnell* |
| Green Woodwork | *Mike Abbott* |
| A Guide to Work-Holding on the Lathe | *Fred Holder* |
| Keith Rowley's Woodturning Projects | *Keith Rowley* |
| Making Screw Threads in Wood | *Fred Holder* |
| Segmented Turning: A Complete Guide | *Ron Hampton* |
| Turned Boxes: 50 Designs | *Chris Stott* |
| Turning Green Wood | *Michael O'Donnell* |
| Turning Pens and Pencils | *Kip Christensen & Rex Burningham* |
| Wood for Woodturners | *Mark Baker* |
| Woodturning: Forms and Materials | *John Hunnex* |

Woodturning: A Foundation Course (New Edition)                    Keith Rowley
Woodturning: A Fresh Approach                                     Robert Chapman
Woodturning: An Individual Approach                              Dave Regester
Woodturning: A Source Book of Shapes                             John Hunnex
Woodturning Masterclass                                          Tony Boase
Woodturning Projects: A Workshop Guide to Shapes                Mark Baker

## Woodworking

Beginning Picture Marquetry                                Lawrence Threadgold
Carcass Furniture                                            GMC Publications
Celtic Carved Lovespoons: 30 Patterns          Sharon Littley & Clive Griffin
Celtic Woodcraft                                             Glenda Bennett
Celtic Woodworking Projects                                  Glenda Bennett
Complete Woodfinishing (Revised Edition)                     Ian Hosker
David Charlesworth's Furniture-Making Techniques            David Charlesworth
David Charlesworth's Furniture-Making Techniques – Volume 2   David Charlesworth
Furniture Projects with the Router                           Kevin Ley
Furniture Restoration (Practical Crafts)                    Kevin Jan Bonner
Furniture Restoration: A Professional at Work                John Lloyd
Furniture Workshop                                           Kevin Ley
Green Woodwork                                               Mike Abbott
History of Furniture: Ancient to 1900                       Michael Huntley
Intarsia: 30 Patterns for the Scrollsaw                      John Everett
Making Heirloom Boxes                                        Peter Lloyd
Making Screw Threads in Wood                                 Fred Holder
Making Woodwork Aids and Devices                            Robert Wearing
Mastering the Router                                         Ron Fox
Pine Furniture Projects for the Home                        Dave Mackenzie
Router Magic: Jigs, Fixtures and Tricks to Unleash your Router's Full Potential
                                                            Bill Hylton
Router Projects for the Home                                 GMC Publications
Router Tips & Techniques                                    Robert Wearing
Routing: A Workshop Handbook                                Anthony Bailey
Routing for Beginners (Revised and Expanded Edition)        Anthony Bailey
Stickmaking: A Complete Course                    Andrew Jones & Clive George
Stickmaking Handbook                              Andrew Jones & Clive George
Storage Projects for the Router                              GMC Publications
Success with Sharpening                                      Ralph Laughton
Veneering: A Complete Course                                Ian Hosker
Veneering Handbook                                          Ian Hosker
Wood: Identification & Use                                  Terry Porter
Woodworking Techniques and Projects                         Anthony Bailey
Woodworking with the Router: Professional
     Router Techniques any Woodworker can Use      Bill Hylton & Fred Matlack

## Upholstery

| | |
|---|---|
| The Upholsterer's Pocket Reference Book | *David James* |
| Upholstery: A Complete Course (Revised Edition) | *David James* |
| Upholstery Restoration | *David James* |
| Upholstery Techniques & Projects | *David James* |
| Upholstery Tips and Hints | *David James* |

## Dolls' Houses and Miniatures

| | |
|---|---|
| 1/12 Scale Character Figures for the Dolls' House | *James Carrington* |
| Americana in 1/12 Scale: 50 Authentic Projects | *Joanne Ogreenc & Mary Lou Santovec* |
| The Authentic Georgian Dolls' House | *Brian Long* |
| A Beginners' Guide to the Dolls' House Hobby | *Jean Nisbett* |
| Celtic, Medieval and Tudor Wall Hangings in 1/12 Scale Needlepoint | |
| | *Sandra Whitehead* |
| Creating Decorative Fabrics: Projects in 1/12 Scale | *Janet Storey* |
| Dolls' House Accessories, Fixtures and Fittings | *Andrea Barham* |
| Dolls' House Furniture: Easy-to-Make Projects in 1/12 Scale | *Freida Gray* |
| Dolls' House Makeovers | *Jean Nisbett* |
| Dolls' House Window Treatments | *Eve Harwood* |
| Edwardian-Style Hand-Knitted Fashion for 1/12 Scale Dolls | *Yvonne Wakefield* |
| How to Make Your Dolls' House Special: Fresh Ideas for Decorating | *Beryl Armstrong* |
| Making 1/12 Scale Wicker Furniture for the Dolls' House | *Sheila Smith* |
| Making Miniature Chinese Rugs and Carpets | *Carol Phillipson* |
| Making Miniature Food and Market Stalls | *Angie Scarr* |
| Making Miniature Gardens | *Freida Gray* |
| Making Miniature Oriental Rugs & Carpets | *Meik & Ian McNaughton* |
| Making Miniatures: Projects for the 1/12 Scale Dolls' House | *Christiane Berridge* |
| Making Period Dolls' House Accessories | *Andrea Barham* |
| Making Tudor Dolls' Houses | *Derek Rowbottom* |
| Making Upholstered Furniture in 1/12 Scale | *Janet Storey* |
| Medieval and Tudor Needlecraft: Knights and Ladies in 1/12 Scale | *Sandra Whitehead* |
| Miniature Bobbin Lace | *Roz Snowden* |
| Miniature Crochet: Projects in 1/12 Scale | *Roz Walters* |
| Miniature Embroidered Patchwork: Projects in 1/12 Scale | *Margaret Major* |
| Miniature Embroidery for the Georgian Dolls' House | *Pamela Warner* |
| Miniature Embroidery for the Tudor and Stuart Dolls' House | *Pamela Warner* |
| Miniature Embroidery for the 20th-Century Dolls' House | *Pamela Warner* |
| Miniature Embroidery for the Victorian Dolls' House | *Pamela Warner* |
| Miniature Needlepoint Carpets | *Janet Granger* |
| The Modern Dolls' House | *Jean Nisbett* |
| More Miniature Oriental Rugs & Carpets | *Meik & Ian McNaughton* |
| Needlepoint 1/12 Scale: Design Collections for the Dolls' House | *Felicity Price* |
| New Ideas for Miniature Bobbin Lace | *Roz Snowden* |
| Patchwork Quilts for the Dolls' House: 20 Projects in 1/12 Scale | *Sarah Williams* |

## Gardening

## Photography

## Art Techniques

# Videos

| | |
|---|---|
| Drop-in and Pinstuffed Seats | *David James* |
| Stuffover Upholstery | *David James* |
| Elliptical Turning | *David Springett* |
| Woodturning Wizardry | *David Springett* |
| Turning Between Centres: The Basics | *Dennis White* |
| Turning Bowls | *Dennis White* |
| Boxes, Goblets and Screw Threads | *Dennis White* |
| Novelties and Projects | *Dennis White* |
| Classic Profiles | *Dennis White* |
| Twists and Advanced Turning | *Dennis White* |
| Sharpening the Professional Way | *Jim Kingshott* |
| Sharpening Turning & Carving Tools | *Jim Kingshott* |
| Bowl Turning | *John Jordan* |
| Hollow Turning | *John Jordan* |
| Woodturning: A Foundation Course | *Keith Rowley* |
| Carving a Figure: The Female Form | *Ray Gonzalez* |
| The Router: A Beginner's Guide | *Alan Goodsell* |
| The Scroll Saw: A Beginner's Guide | *John Burke* |

# Magazines

**WOODTURNING ◆ WOODCARVING ◆ FURNITURE & CABINETMAKING
THE ROUTER ◆ NEW WOODWORKING ◆ THE DOLLS' HOUSE MAGAZINE
OUTDOOR PHOTOGRAPHY ◆ BLACK & WHITE PHOTOGRAPHY
KNITTING ◆ ORGANIC LIFE ◆ GUILD NEWS**

The above represents a full list of all titles currently published or scheduled
to be published. All are available direct from the Publishers or through
bookshops, newsagents and specialist retailers.
To place an order, or to obtain a complete catalogue, contact:

**GMC PUBLICATIONS,
166 High Street, Lewes,
East Sussex BN7 1XU United Kingdom
Tel: 01273 488005  Fax: 01273 478606
E-mail: pubs@thegmcgroup.com
Website: www.gmcpubs.com**

*Orders by credit card are accepted*